My Mother's Last Days

The Story of Sally Faderan's Last Days

MARY FADERAN

Copyright © 2018 Mary Faderan

ISBN-13: 978-0-692-11309-7

ISBN-10: 0-692-11309-6

All rights reserved.

DEDICATION

To my dear Mom, Sally, who sacrificed throughout her life and met so much adversity. To her vivacity and beauty and loveliness. Being with her was like heaven and I miss her always.

CONTENTS

	Acknowledgments	i
1	Foreword	ii
2	December 2010	1
3	January 2011	6
4	February 2011	40
5	March 2011	100

ACKNOWLEDGMENTS

I am deeply indebted to God and His Divine Providence. I do not intend to use this book to gain anything other than to let those who are interested know that God has the Last Answer.

MARY FADERAN

FOREWORD

This book is seven years too late in the making. I was contemplating my Mom's life one afternoon and decided that it might be a good idea to write about her last days. Those days were the worst in her life and in the life of her family. But that will become apparent later on in this book.

Sally Faderan was a retired teacher. She taught all grades all the way up to college level. I remember her teaching high school in the province of Dagupan, Philippines at the local Catholic high school. She taught English and gave plays where her class would perform poetry and dramas. I wanted so much to be with her class and not be in my kindergarten class, it was that much fun to be with her. Mom also taught in the public college of Philippines SBA, a city college. She taught a lot of courses including a course on Marriage. Many students flocked to listen to her talk. And many returned to sign up for a repeat course just to keep listening to her talk about life as a married woman. She was very much admired, and very much sought after, even though she was a very humble woman who did not have much in terms of fortune or real fame.

Mom grew up during the last War. The Japanese occupied her home town. The children were taught Japanese and she learned a few words. Those words came to her rescue when once she and a couple of classmates were rendered speechless as they stared at the business end of a bayonet trained at them by a Japanese soldier. She said something to the soldier and he let them free. Mom used to recount stories of being driven out of her home and walking endlessly through rice fields and mountains with her loving Aunt, Gregoria V. Duque, and sleeping under the stars wondering if things would ever be back to normal again.

She was raised from infancy by Gregoria, whom she loving called Maman and who also helped to raise me. Gregoria was Canuto's sister who never married. She was a devotee of St. Anthony and I remember seeing her at the window every afternoon, dressed in Brown and praying the rosary waiting for her dear Salud (Mom's legal first name) to come home from work. When my grandfather remarried Mom went to live with him and his new wife and grew up with her half siblings, a boy and two girls.

My Mom was an English major at University of Santo Tomas (UST), Philippines. Mom worked part time at the bookstore, cheerfully accepting the fact that money from home would be scarce.

MOM'S LAST DAYS

Her stepmother was jealous of her and kept away from her the happiness she could have had with her father, who had married her mother and lost her to death when Mom was a mere infant.

Her life was full and joyful, despite the sacrifices of living a good and holy, Catholic vocation as a married woman and mother to me, her only living child. Mom was a great cook. She loved to watch the cooking shows on TV. She wanted me to download all of the recipes that she liked to try on us. Many times I'd go home for lunch and to my – er – consternation, wanted me to eat the food she made and not be starving for the rest of the day. Consternation, I say, because she made me stay and not fidget about having to rush back to work. She was also able to whip up recipes like this chocolate fudge cake that she got from a Food and Wine magazine. Her egg rolls were legend. Her summer pasta salad was a comfort food to me and my Dad. She made lovely recipes that were so good and nutritious.

She likes to recount the day when she met my Dad. He was a law student at the university. A handsome man who liked music and played the piano without having any training. He could duplicate a tune and make everyone shimmy and sway. That afternoon, one of her friends saw her and said: "Wait here! I want you to meet someone!" Her friend rushed away and then returned, with my Dad in tow. They met and then history was made then and there. Dad traveled a long distance by train to ask her hand in marriage. He endured the stifling atmosphere of the train with all kinds of passengers. Passengers who brought unlikely companions with them – chickens and all sorts of animals. But he was determined to marry her.

Their engagement was agreed upon by both their fathers, who had been great friends without their children knowing

MOM'S LAST DAYS

about it. Her father was Canuto Duque
and his father was Nemesio Faderan Sr.
Canuto was also a teacher like Mom.
Nemesio was a lawyer, like my Dad.

Their courtship was good. Mom liked to
recount how when he came to visit her,
Mom's aunt would sprinkle salt on his
collar to give him the hint that he had
overstayed. Mom and Dad were engaged
through her school as an English major at
UST. Then she took a year to teach at a
rather secluded island somewhere in the
Philippines. My Dad wasn't thrilled and
wrote her all the time. She wrote really
good letters. His letters to her are now
unknown in location.

When they married, they looked so very
happy. Shy and smiling at the camera. Or
not at the camera but at someone else out
of shot. Mom married Dad at Lourdes
Church, Quezon City.

MARY FADERAN

They had me in 1956. Three miscarriages ensued after I was born. It was a sad occasion for each. They, my siblings, were named Vicente, Chris (unknown gender) and Gregory. My mother went to Medjugorje sometime in the '90's and went to receive the Sacrament of Reconciliation there. The priest suggested that she name her miscarried children and so she did. I believe that my siblings are in Heaven but they are so hidden and now Mom is with them.

My Mom was a stay-at-home mom while I was still in diapers and until I was in grade school. After a while, she taught in my school but was never my teacher. I remember Mom sitting with all the Moms while I attended grade school. Once I recall walking down the street from school with her, and we peeked into a bookstore and that was a treat.

MOM'S LAST DAYS

Mom, Dad and I moved to the USA in 1970. She received a work visa to be one of the teachers the USA needed at that time. There was a shortage of teachers then. My father was working at the time 'in the field' where he opened Social Security branches throughout the provinces in Northern Luzon. So Mom wasn't thrilled with that and actually went to see President Marcos one Christmas Morning when he and his wife, Imelda, held an outdoor reception for all the voters to meet them. My Mom wrote a short letter outlining what she wanted the President to do for her. In the letter she explained the situation, and proposed that Marcos arrange for my Dad to come back to a more stable position in Manila. When she took a cab and went in line to shake the President's hand, she said that she relieved that she did write a letter. When time came to meet the President, she gave him her letter with a short preamble and he shook her hand and handed her letter to his aide. My Mom left and went home, hoping for the best. My Mom liked to say that she couldn't even have a decent argument with my Dad because of his long absences.

My father returned home early one week and asked her why was he called back so soon. Mom did not really explain. My father realized after meeting with his boss that he was being given a permanent position at the office. Mom was happy and our lives seemed to flow from there. But in the meantime, Mom had a conversation with one of her distant relatives who was also our family doctor. He suggested that she apply for a visa to the USA as there was a teacher shortage then. My Mom did this and waited also for any news. It didn't happen overnight and the return of my Dad coincided with this USA visa plan. We didn't find out till around 1969 or so that we were given a visa. We left in 1970. Mom went first and joined friends in Hawaii, where she took a part time job at a mall as a clerk. My Dad and I followed after I was finished with school. We visited in Hawaii with our friends and then with Mom, flew to LA to visit one of her school teacher friends over the July 4 weekend. We flew to Indianapolis and met my Aunt, Mary Lagadon who took us in to stay with her family until we could find a place to live and work and go to school.

Mom taught at the St. Lawrence School teaching 6th grade for many years. Dad worked at a title company. I went to high school at Ladywood-St. Agnes near our apartment at Park Forest Drive.

When I graduated school I moved to Hamden, CT and worked at Yale School of Medicine. My father became unemployed during Reagan's tenure in the White House and was persuaded to move to New York to find a better job. Mom taught at the St. Sebastian School in Woodside, NY. Dad worked for different title companies in New York City and in Long Island. I joined them in 1987 when I moved to New York to work at Memorial Sloan Kettering Cancer Center to work for a cancer oncologist who moved his lab from Yale.

MARY FADERAN

We lived in Woodside for the 4 years I was at Sloan Kettering. Our life there was not always exciting in the best way. Once while I was still in Connecticut, my parents were robbed in daylight. Her pearls and Dad's good camera were stolen. She wasn't that happy but it was life in New York. Their first apartment was a cramped second floor two bedroom. I hardly recall it but remember the low ceiling in my bedroom. We moved to a better place in 6128 Broadway, close to the R train and walking distance from the 7 train. Our first floor neighbors, the Lopezes, were a retired couple who owne the building. We lived on the second floor and had a nice view of the street and ample noise from the subway and the La Guardia Airport. We had a good life in a way – but we were tried by many ups and downs as life happened there. When I was ready to move on in my career, I decided to have us all move back to Indiana where we felt more secure and had friends.

Mom retired from teaching while at New York and worked for a medical doctor's

MOM'S LAST DAYS

wife in Park Avenue. Mom also worked for Optifast, a diet company in Manhattan. Mom wasn't thrilled living in New York and yet, because she was a faithful and dutiful and loving wife, she accompanied my Dad with all of their belongings in a U-haul to move there. She was stalwart, though, and made the best of things. Her idea of riding a subway was a bit much and so she stayed in the area where many times, students of hers would run into her after school or weekends as she did some shopping. Her students loved her there and she loved them too. When she was told by her supervisor one day during her review that she doing well, but could no longer keep her employed, my Mom was surprised and disappointed. She left and went to another school which was about as pleasant as a day in Hell to work in. Her last day was when she almost got boxed in the ears by a rebellious kid. When she went to the Principal's office to complain, the Principal took the kid's side. Mom said she was quitting then and there and walked away.

MARY FADERAN

We moved back to Indiana in 1991 where I took a position at the School of Veterinary Medicine at Purdue University in West Lafayette, Indiana. My Dad and Mom retired there, however, Dad took a part time job at the Tippecanoe Title in Lafayette. My Mom was a part time tutor to three children of a Filipino family and after she was finished teaching for the day, she went to hear Mass at the Precious Blood Monastery next door on State Street. My Dad or I would accompany her there and enjoyed the friendship and fellowship of the others who attended.

In Indiana once again, we enjoyed the cozy life of a family that cared for each other and kept each other's company. My Mom loved to write articles for the newsletter of the church group she belonged to – Schoenstatt of Indiana; cook good food, and sing with my Dad while he played our piano. She loved to entertain when there was a reason for it.

MOM'S LAST DAYS

Mom was a social person and liked to talk with her numerous friends and family on the phone. She made many friends in Indiana and many of the Filipino students at Purdue enjoyed occasional parties with her as a guest or host. Mom also started a Rosary group in Lafayette. She grew in her faith in our second life here in Indiana. Being a stay at home wife and Mom again, she was able to grow in her Love for God and His Mother. She enjoyed watching EWTN, Mother Angelica's shows, and read a vast number of books about Catholicism.

Her life was great and yet humble. But she suffered a lot from physical infirmities as she grew older. She suffered frequent eye infections – tearing from one eye and not the other; skin ailments that seemed to defy diagnosis but was cleared up by steroids; foot problems; osteoporosis; dental issues which made it hard for her to eat well. She seemed so inundated with difficult physical stresses and it was hard for us to watch her suffer.

She saw a dermatologist in Indianapolis who was the only one she trusted. The ones in the city were not good enough as they seemed indifferent to her calls to ask for help. Her dermatologist in Indianapolis was a nice Irish doctor who was an ex-Navy man. There were many weeks that went by when she had to come to see him to get rid of this skin ailment. Not able to drive, she asked us to take her there and we always were happy to go there to see her doctor. After she saw him and got treated, we would go to the Mall and have a snack or browse.

Mom loved to shop and so did I. We would go for hours to look at Macy's, or Von Maur, or Nordstrom while Dad stayed seated at a chair looking at his cell phone or even dozing until we came back to his side ready for us to drive back home. Mom also liked to watch QVC where she

MOM'S LAST DAYS

enjoyed watching the beautiful hosts who offered jewelry and clothes and cooking utensils.

The most enjoyable times for me was just being with Mom and Dad as she commandeered the remote and switched the TV stations from QVC, HSN and Food Network. I am sure that this sounds very boring to you, but for us, it was pretty much a cosy evening.

In her later years, Mom snoozed a lot. She also spent a long morning at prayer. She had an altar to the Sacred Heart of Jesus over the piano and another altar to the Mother Thrice Admirable of Schoenstatt on another wall. She was a devout follower of St. Padre Pio. Mom also went to see Pope John Paul II when he visited sometime in the '90's. One of her friends recounted that my Mom stood on top of her folding chair to wave to the Pope as he passed by. She had held the icon of the

MARY FADERAN

Mother Thrice Admirable aloft for him to bless.

Once, Mom went on a Pilgrimage to Medjugorje where she was accompanied by one of her friends, Ann. Mom had an adventure of sorts there. She was about to board when the ticket person said she couldn't find her on the roster of passengers. Mom was surprised and after further investigation, the ticket person found her in the First Class section. My Mom said that she figured out why: She was carrying with her the Mother Thrice Admirable icon and that was why she got to sit at the best seat in the plane. Her devotion to Our Blessed Mother was so deep. She loved Jesus very much and sat numerous Monday evenings at the Adoration chapel praying the Rosary. She said all three mysteries many times, and frequently prayed the Divine Mercy chaplet.

MOM'S LAST DAYS

This book is intended for those who ever wondered what ever happened to her while she suffered her last days. While Mom had a very difficult but happy life in serving God, her ability to endure is only now to be recounted and this book shows how her suffering was so great that re-reading these emails reminds me in a profound way how the elderly become so much a victim of their circumstances.

I hope that those who read it will see the difficult process of dying and how her last days are captured for posterity.

DECEMBER 2010

December 2, 2010

Hi Holly,

Could you please ask for prayers for my Mom who's got this Achilles tendon pain and redness. For her doctor to give her the treatment that will heal her.

Also pray for Amy's daughter who is getting married this coming Sunday (Dec 5) - that the marriage will be blessed with

MARY FADERAN

many years of joy and happiness and the gift of life.

Also - thanksgiving for a good resolution to a work-related problem.

God bless and thanks,

Mary

December 3, 2010

Hello Holly/Kathy,

Please pray for:

Mom's healing of her Achilles tendon

Repose of Gerry Robinos, Sr. who died yesterday unexpectedly. For his family and friends who are mourning his loss.

MOM'S LAST DAYS

Thanks & God bless!

December 3, 2010

Hello Janine and Carole,

I just saw the weather forecast for tomorrow. I am concerned that it will be quite hazardous to travel

through 25 to Delphi for the Schoenstatt Event. I don't know if Mom has spoken or called you lately, but

she has an inflamed Achilles tendon and she may not be able to walk without pain. I don't think that I can leave my Mom by herself either to drive with my Dad. I am worried for my Dad driving in the bad weather especially since he is not that young anymore and his vision is limited (especially in the dark road of 25).

Please advise me so that perhaps a solution can be formulated. I'd rather spare my Dad driving in the wintry mix.

Thanks very much!

Mary

December 4, 2010

Hi Susana,

Thanks for your email. I just got up a few minutes ago and my parents are still asleep. I don't know if Mom is able to

walk much (she has an inflamed Achilles tendon) but she has been on antibiotics for a day so far. When they awake I will tell them of your invitation. Thank you for inviting us. I just saw the white snow outside.

God bless,

Mary

MOM'S LAST DAYS

December 6, 2010

Mary dear, Lynn called and told me that Dr W ordered the changed and will call Walmart for a new one (sounds like "rack"). I'll start it tomorrow. Take care... Mom

Sent via BlackBerry by AT&T

December 20, 2010

Hello Holly/Kathy,

Please continue prayers for my Mom. Her heel and ankle are still sore and red and she's already done with her antibiotics. She is going to Sigma this morning to have them take a look. Please pray for healing and proper treatment. Thanks!

God bless,

MARY FADERAN

Mary

December 29, 2010

Hi Holly,

Please continue to pray that my Mom's foot gets better. The dermatologist said it's a serious infection and gave her more antibiotics. She will see her GP and foot dr next week. Also pls pray that we can make a wise decision to change her dr to one who is an internist.

Thanks and God bless!

Mary

JANUARY 2011

January 2, 2011

Hi Holly,

Please continue prayers for Mom as she has developed an infection on her foot. She is on antibiotics and is due to see a foot dr on Monday.

Please pray for good medical care and healing.

Thanks,

Mary

MARY FADERAN

MOM'S LAST DAYS

January 3, 2011

Hello Everyone,

Just a request please to pray for Mom. She saw the foot doctor this afternoon due to heel pain. The doctor said she has critical limb ischemia secondary to peripheral artery disease. She will go to St Elizabeth on Wednesday afternoon so that they can run a test on her. The doctor took Doppler readings on her foot to see if she has any pulses. One of her pulses was good but another one (on the side of the foot) was reading zero.

We're not sure where this will go but I've been reading a little about the treatment and the one that seems to work is putting a stent in. Also the literature seems to point to other types of treatment like meds to decrease the plaque, etc.

Thanks so much in advance for the prayers. Mom is currently preparing her Schoenstatt article that she sends out monthly. She said that the pain is not as bad now, so that is good. The heel is still purplish.

The doctor says that it is purple due to lack of blood flow, and also the pain is due to the same thing.

Blessings,

Mary

Hi Ding,

Thanks for the prayers, Ding.
Unfortunately, one of the drawbacks from this affliction can be the loss of a limb. We do not want that to happen. It is a difficult time for Mom and Dad and me, but we are trusting in God's providence, healing and protection.

Blessings,

Mary

MOM'S LAST DAYS

January 4, 2011

Hi,

Please pray for my Mom. The doctor diagnosed her heel pain as critical limb ischemia. He was able to detect one pulse in her foot but not the other. Mom will go to the hospital for testing tomorrow. Then next Wed the foot doctor will see her to explain test results.

I'm hoping it can be cured. We are really trusting in God's care and need as many prayers.

I'll keep you posted.

Love,

Agnes/Ate

January 4, 2011

MARY FADERAN

Dear Fr Stan,

Could do you pray for my Mom Sally? She has this purple heel and has pain. The foot dr said she has critical limb ischemia. They will do testing on her leg pulses tomorrow. Please pray for a good prognosis and safe and effective treatment.

Thank you!

Mary

MOM'S LAST DAYS

January 4, 2011

Hi Dan,

I just had a question. Do you have any ideas on what a person can do to recover (outside of surgery or angioplasty) from peripheral artery disease? I am asking because my Mom just recently had a foot problem and the foot doctor (Conway) tested her yesterday. He diagnosed her as having critical limb ischemia secondary to PAD. My Mom will undergo some more tests tomorrow, and will see Dr Conway next week to get the results.

If you have any suggestions, I'm very interested to find out.

Thanks and Happy New Year.

Mary

January 4, 2011

Hello Everyone,

Just an update. I got a call from her doctor today when I got home for lunch. When Mom goes for her test tomorrow they will keep her overnight and give her fluids in preparation for the radiology procedure they plan for her on Thursday. The interventional radiologist is going to remove the blockage on her artery.

Please continue to pray that the procedure is successful and safe.

I'll keep everyone posted with more as it goes.

Thanks again for your prayers,

Mary

January 4, 2011

Hi Holly,

MOM'S LAST DAYS

Please pray for a successful procedure that will be performed to remove the blockage in my Mom's leg/foot this Thursday. Pray that my Mom will be strong and tolerate the treatment.

Thanks,

Mary

January 4, 2011

Dear Rheeda,

Thanks so much! We appreciate your prayers always.

I'm glad that the doctors are moving quickly to help Mom. I came home today and helped Mom with bandaging her heel. I was very concerned to see that her toes are so white. I had called her MD's office earlier today and left a message, and so I was getting worried that they had not yet called back. But, the phone rang and it was her MD and she wanted to tell me the plans for Mom's procedure. The doc said that she is going to be given fluids so that her kidneys will tolerate the dye they will use. I looked up her radiologist online and he (if that is him) seems to be pretty sharp.

Mom is bearing all this sweetly, and a little bit dazedly, but she called some of her friends in Indy (Tita Dely Dicen) who had advised her that she needs to be active so that her circulation will be increased. I'm hoping that Mom can go back to the gym (she's been out of the gym for a couple of years now) so that she can resume walking on the treadmill. Or, we might just get a second hand treadmill and put it in our third bedroom so that both of them (and me) can use it.

Must go, thanks and hugs/kisses!

Mary

January 5, 2011

Hello Rheeda,

MOM'S LAST DAYS

Many thanks for your prayers. I am with Mom and Dad in her room at the Observation center watching EWTN. One of Mom's favorite nuns is on and she is Sr Briege McKenna.

She got through her test and met her hospitalist and radiologist already. They have not told us when she is having her procedure tomorrow. But we hope that they will let us know before Dad and I go home.

I showed Mom your email. Maybe she will write you later.

I talked to one of our sales mgrs at work who is familiar with the procedure and I felt more relieved that the process is routine. He said that his Dad has had similar procedures also.

Dad and I went to the cafeteria after I got in from work. Mom already had her dinner. They serve good meals here.

Another plus is they have wifi.

I will send you an email once we know when her procedure will be.

Love,

Mary

Hi Holly,

Please pray for a successful procedure that will be performed to remove the blockage in my Mom's leg/foot this Thursday. Pray that my Mom will be strong and tolerate the treatment.

Thanks,

Mary

January 6, 2011

Hello Everyone,

You may have seen my post on FB, but in case you aren't on FB, Mom is now out of the IR procedure room. She's resting now,

MOM'S LAST DAYS

and sleepy, and they put in 2 stents in her leg. Her heel looks remarkably good, and she seems to still have pain when you touch it. I think it may not be 100 percent but it is pretty darn close. She will stay overnight one more time so they can keep an eye on her labs etc. and then tomorrow she will go home. I think that they will probably make her get on a walking program to keep her from getting this way again. We shall see what her doctors say.

Thank you very much for your prayers. I'm sure that kept everything going well.

Best regards,

Mary

January 6, 2011

Hello Rheeda,

Many thanks for your prayers. I am with Mom and Dad in her room at the Observation center watching EWTN. One of Mom's favorite nuns is on and she is Sr Briege McKenna.

She got through her test and met her hospitalist and radiologist already. They have not told us when she is having her procedure tomorrow. But we hope that they will let us know before Dad and I go home.

I showed Mom your email. Maybe she will write you later.

I talked to one of our sales mgrs at work who is familiar with the procedure and I felt more relieved that the process is routine. He said that his Dad has had similar procedures also.

Dad and I went to the cafeteria after I got in from work. Mom already had her dinner. They serve good meals here. Another plus is they have wifi.

I will send you an email once we know when her procedure will be.

Love,
Mary

MOM'S LAST DAYS

January 6, 2011

Dear Julia,

She just came back from and her Dr said they
put two stents. She is a little
sleepy but stable. Her foot looks great although
she says it is still
painful. However we think it will heal in time.

We are told she needs to stay flat for 4 hours
and then stay overnight so
they can take her labs. She should go home
tomorrow in the early afternoon.

Again we thank you for your prayers. Our
family is much relieved. It was so
hard to see her suffering this pain not realizing
what the cause was till
last Monday. I am sure we will make certain
she gets a walking program and
sticks to it.

In Jesus,
Mary and family

MARY FADERAN

January 6, 2011

Hello Ann,

Right now we are with Mom in her room watching the news. We are just so glad and relieved. Today was hard but I

did not feel so because I knew people were praying. Thank you. My Mom is just very glad too. I think we definitely

need to make sure that all three of us make the effort to be more active. I will be interested to know how Mom's drs will have her get more active.

I went to work this afternoon and got some things done. My boss was glad about the news. He likes my Mom and his wife does too.

Tomorrow we bring Mom home. She will take Plavix. I read up on it and they say to make sure not to get cuts bec of bleeding. That is a concern.

This weekend is our Franciscan meetings

MOM'S LAST DAYS

onSat [sic] and Sun. Block rosary Sat and Mom's Christmas exchange with her

Schoenstatt group on Sun. Busy. She might be still too tired but maybe she should go since she needs to be active.

I cannot believe it is Friday tomorrow. I sure will be glad for that!

How are you feeling now? Get some rest and keep warm! You need to take care of yourself.

Well, I will say so long for now.

Take care and God bless!

Mary

January 7, 2011

She is going home today but not before she gets a blood transfusion. She's been anemic so that is the reason. Thank you for your prayers. We are glad that God took care of her and gave her a renewed limb.

Love,

Agnes

January 7, 2011

Hi Marilu,

Thank you so much for your prayers. I believe that our prayers have made a big difference in how well she responded to the treatment.

You are welcome to visit anytime. I don't think we have any plans to be out of town next week. We do have adoration on Monday evening, but that is the only evening we are out of the house.

MOM'S LAST DAYS

Please do come and visit. She has been cooped up in St E for three days now and would love to have you to chat with:-)

Thanks again,

Mary

January 7, 2011

Hello Ann,

I am concerned that you are still feeling ill. Please see your dr. You can never be too sure about these things. My Mom had this foot problem since November 29th and we were under the impression it was plantar fasciitis since her Dr had told that before sometime back. Then my Mom had to badger her doctor's nurse to tell her dr about how it wasn't getting better. And her dermatologist had said before it was poor circulation but did not get through to us then. So get yourself checked out. I don't want to scare you, but you know with age things just have a way of getting bogged down. My Mom and I are considering having her seen by an internist now. I was with my Mom at her last Drs appointment and the doctor just did not focus at all on my Mom's pain and that was already in December 20th. She just focused on the swelling. She said to wear those support hose. Now, I am sure that if it were an internist or someone who was more familiar with these ailments, Mom would be doing a lot better by now. So I feel really unhappy about how it went for a longer time than it should have. Just very unhappy.

But, now that Mom's leg has been treated and she sounds good (over the phone, since I am at work still) it should be ok. Her foot doctor will see her next week and then the main dr the week after (she went to a medical mission). Her appointment with my internist is not till the 25th. I think maybe we can still go to that one. I know it is hard to fire a doctor but when it is as

MOM'S LAST DAYS

important as one's life, it is really needed, I think. What do you think? I don't know right now still. We have the appointment still set for that date.

My work is getting done and thanks be to God. I am getting some good feedback from those who are above me in the hierarchy. The clinical manager, Jay, just read my work and he likes it. He may just become my boss once Perry retires. And, I am glad about that because I sure don't want the stress of being a boss, you know?

Well, it is Friday and I sure don't feel like it is Friday. Seems like I'm on a roll and cannot sit back and relax for some reason. Did you know that I have signed up to train for a 5K? It is a program at work. I think I can do it, but you never know till you get to the race. I hope and pray that I can train. I ran around our neighborhood last Sunday (and the Friday before that) when the weather was 29 degrees. I could do it. I did have times when I walked, but I jogged more lengthily than walked. happy about this. And I am not getting too sore afterwards and that is so good. I am reading a Nutrition for Runners book. They state that if one is having soreness after a workout it is possible that the diet is lacking protein and/or fat.

That is interesting because I eat a low fat type diet. Sometimes when Mom makes something with fried foods, I eat that or we get something from a fast food. But perhaps this little info is helpful. I don't know if I told you that I have been taking selenium. My internist said my labs for thyroid seem to be low so she will retest me in a few weeks. I hope that my thyroid is normal. But it might not be, since Mom's is also hypo. It runs in the family, I think.

Well, Mom is getting transfused right now. They won't get done till about six pm. So I am going to the WalMart after work to pick up her Plavix. I learned it is a bit expensive. But, hopefully this is not so bad after Medicare coverage.

Must get going then. I do hope you feel better soon. Have fun with your

MOM'S LAST DAYS

grandchild.

Love and prayers,

Mary

January 9, 2011

Dear Bassy, Lenie et family,

Your prayers are very much appreciated. She is still having some pain. But she is doing better.

Love,

Agnes

January 10, 2011

Dear Sister Ann,

Thank you so much for your email and for

your offering a Mass for Mom. She is still having a little pain when her heel is touched. I had called the nurse that assisted her radiologist last week on Mom's procedure to ask him whether this is to be expected. He said that this is what they call "reperfusion pain" when the blood finally gets to reach the places where it could not before. He said that if she is still having this in a couple of days to call him back. He also gave me his direct line to be reached sooner. His words give me much relief as it is difficult to see Mom still having a pain. I am sure though, that she is on the road to recovery. Your prayers on her behalf are much welcomed!

She did get to go to Mass yesterday, although it was later in the day since she didn't think she could go to the usual Mass time. She does get around on her feet at home and sometimes with a cane, but usually not. She did get a little work done - preparing a meal. I had cautioned her to not lie down so much so that her foot might be given ample opportunity to have the blood flowing down her leg.

MOM'S LAST DAYS

Yes, her whole life is a beautiful offering to God. I believe that God has a special love for my Mom. It is so inspiring and she is always so loving.

Thank you again, Sr Ann. God bless you always:-)

Love,

Mary

January 10, 2011

Hello Ann,

Great to hear from you and that you are feeling much better.

I had to call Mom's radiologist office today since I was still having concerns and finally spoke to Jesse, the radiology nurse. He said that what my Mom is feeling (pain) is due to "reperfusion" and that is when the blood returns to the formerly unperfused area and causing the nerves to be more sensitive. He said that if it doesn't go away in the next couple of days to call back. He gave me his direct number and was very helpful. I am glad that I finally called someone. I called the podiatrist's office but they were not able to give me any advice except to tell me to call her doctor (who is out of town!).

Well, I will surely have Mom see my internist. The only thing is that she is from Clarian Arnett and does not have privileges (or won't) at St E. I think that with her being an internist, I think that will be ok. I told my internist that I won't go to Clarian but only to St E. We will see her on the 25th.

Mom was able to go to Mass yesterday. She does still use a cane to walk around. She is very enthused about Facebook and likes to comment of people's posts. It's fun to watch how she likes to write on FB.

Yes, we have been so stressed. Last

MOM'S LAST DAYS

Thursday I didn't think I could handle it. I tried to call Dr B but he is out of town until this week. I decided to just pray hard and also I wrote the National Centre for Padre Pio and they said they are putting my Mom's name to Padre Pio's gloves. Somehow we went through it. I guess I am glad that we did get through it. Thanks be to God!

So this week we are just going to take it easy. At least not going anywhere. It will snow tomorrow early and throughout the day. Maybe get 4-6 inches of snow. I asked Dad to cancel his appointment with his dr which is for tomorrow so he doesn't have to drive in that weather. Besides, Dad has been very bad about what he has been eating, and he had not tested his blood sugar for a long time. I finally requested his dr to re-order his blood test strips and got new batteries for his glucometer. Isn't that terrible? He did test his sugar last night and that came back a little high so I warned him that he needs to get back to eating healthy breakfast and not have any cakes or sweet breads. I think that he has been spoiled by the panettone that Mom has been getting from Target and her friend, Nattie has been buying her these since the Christmas season started. So Dad's been eating it for breakfast. He wanted me to buy some more and I said that those aren't regular breads and only come during Christmas.

Now we are surely going to have to behave as well as we can.

We had our Secular Franciscan gathering this weekend (past). We had a prayer service, not sure why, but at least we had a nice one. Then one of us gave a talk about her trip to Assissi [sic]. That was nice.

This coming weekend I am going to have a massage. I don't have any other plans, just rest and get back some breathing space.

Well, I must get back to work. I've counted 7 items to do for this quarter at work. Wish me luck!

MOM'S LAST DAYS

Love and prayers,

Mary

January 10, 2011

Hi Marilu,

Mom is doing well altho with some pain (sensitivity to touch) still. She had 2 visitors today, including Janine.

Yes be careful tomorrow! Mom herself would tell you to come later and be safe from traveling unnecessarily.

I will let her know you plan to visit another day.

Be well and take care,
Mary

MARY FADERAN

January 14, 2011

Hi Marilu,

I know that I haven't replied to your email so I am taking advantage of the lull in the day to update you on Mom's foot.

We had a visit with her podiatrist. He thought that she is going through the healing phase, and that the temperature of her heel has become better than it was and that she needs to have shoes that have the heel part cut out so that she can best walk in them. The podiatrist is a strange type of guy and I don't know if I like him much, but at least that was his conclusion. He offered to look into other ways to help Mom's circulation and mentioned this "roto rooter" type procedure. Mom doesn't like the sound of that as her blood vessels are already quite small and if they do much more rooting about in them they may just fall

MOM'S LAST DAYS

apart! That's why he's not my favorite doctor at this time.

Mom is getting better slowly, and she is keeping up her spirits by daily meditations and prayer. She also likes to go on Facebook to see how her friends are doing. She probably won't be able to make it to Saturday a.m. Mass tomorrow as the snow is going to be coming and it won't be too safe out for her. But, she is going to Sunday Mass, for sure.

We are all very grateful for your prayers, Marilu. These are the best medicines indeed!

I hope that you have a wonderful weekend!

Love,

Mary

January 17, 2011

MARY FADERAN

Hi Holly,

Please pray for good weather on Wed for traveling to doctor's appointment.

Also, thanksgiving for the care and treatment of my Mom when she went to have her procedure done.

Please continue prayers for continued healing and lessening of pain.

Thanksgiving also for all gifts, blessings received.

Please also pray for friends who are either looking for jobs or are in jobs that are toxic.

Prayers for a friend who is in her third trimester, that the baby will be healthy and delivered on time, and for the mother to be healthy also.

Prayers also needed for a man who has two family members suffering from cancer. Prayers for healing and comfort.

For those who have lost loved ones in

MOM'S LAST DAYS

2010, that their journey may be eased by knowledge of God's love and comfort.

I think that is all for now.

Thanks and God bless,

Mary

MARY FADERAN

January 19, 2011 [from my Mom]

Honey,

Pls read Janine's email and send her the things she wants. Tell her I'm on the road.

If you can't do it now do it tonight and I hope I can read what else exactly she wants. Love you!

January 27, 2011

Hi Holly,

I've got a couple of prayer petitions and an update:

1) For Ding who is suffering from a narrowing of the artery leading to his brain - that he will be able to find healing through non-invasive means (he doesn't yet

MOM'S LAST DAYS

want to have an angioplasty).

2) For Cliff who is suffering from a stomach ulcer and for good results of the biopsy of his polyps (from colonoscopy).

3) Update on Mom - her podiatrist says her heel looks significantly better than before her procedure. Thanksgiving for prayers and God's healing grace. Prayers for continued healing and for improved circulation all over.

4) Thanksgiving for good news about a job.

Thanks so much,

Mary

MARY FADERAN

January 31, 2011

Hello Ann,

I do hope that you feel better soon! Yes, there's always that when you think you'll get better. But, from my experience, it is best to have the doctor check you out. Did I tell you last year I had a red spot on the corner of my eye and I didn't like the look of it and when I went to the doctor he said it was an infection and gave me two meds for it, a drop and an ointment.

My Mom went (with us) to her podiatrist yesterday. Her heel looks so much better. The podiatrist actually liked it and said her progress was significantly better. Now he is asking her to think about having stents put into her other leg to head off any problems there. But, Mom and Dad are thinking that maybe they will wait for a while. Her other leg and heel aren't having problems now. It is a lot of stress on Mom to have gone throught [sic] angioplasty this past few weeks. But, the doctor said to let him know when she comes back in 2 weeks.

I got my pu ehr tea yesterday. This tea is supposed to be good for high cholesterol and high fat in the blood. It's from China, in a place called Yunnan province. The tea is pretty good to me in taste, although it has a bit of a smell. My boss' wife is Chinese and she said that it is good too for high blood pressure.

Her grandfather was a medicine man in China and knew all about herbs etc.

I haven't seen Dr B in a really long while. I cancelled our appt last Thursday due to the snow. He said he can see me next week.

I will be seeing my regular MD next week, too. She is watching my thyroid. I do hope that I don't have problems with that. I feel good, right now. The only thing that I notice is that I used to get sore a lot longer after working out, but after I started taking selenium, I haven't had that problem. I read that hypothyroid causes this soreness that lasts longer. However, selenium is supposed to help in the metabolism of thyroid hormone. We shall see if this works for me.

Well, I have a bit of work to do today. I do hope that you have a wonderful weekend. Tomorrow, if it works out, my Mom's wig is going to arrive. We may get it on Saturday.

Love and prayers,

Mary

MOM'S LAST DAYS

January 31, 2011

Hello Ann,

Thank you for your email. I am hoping that you are feeling 100% better today:-) It's good that Don has

been able to help you with things.

We are bracing for a major snow event this week. I postponed Mom's appt with her derma this week

since it will be impossible to drive with all this snow that is supposed to fall over here. She's not too

happy about that as her skin ailment is returning. But, she does feel a little better with her foot, thank

God. She just today went to her regular MD and she was given a med to help restore her appetite. I do hope that it will be effective and safe.

We did not get her wig this past Saturday

as Mom had second thoughts about it. Somehow the effect did not meet with her approval. So we found another wig, and this will be ready for her to pick up this coming Friday. I do hope that this time will do fine.

Our weekend was not too busy as far as social stuff. I did go out to 4 stores yesterday to get groceries, etc. Target was very busy but Marsh and Walmart were as usual, maybe a bit more for a Sunday. Then, at CVS I noticed my right headlight was out so I called Autozone and they had the part. Thank God! The man who helped put the light bulb in my car was nice enough and I'm just grateful not to have to wait for Bob Rohrman to open and so on. I was exhausted when I got home. I did celebrate a little by having some cocoa mix to drink, but then I made a salad that Mom likes (and everyone likes). She says that the taste of garlic/onions, and soy sauce just makes her feel nauseous. I read up on Plavix and that is one of the side effects- nausea. So that was why Mom's dr gave her this new drug.

MOM'S LAST DAYS

I hope that you have a great week ahead.
We plan to go to Adoration tonight but
with this snow coming I am hoping that it
won't hit till after we get home.

Love and prayers,

Mary

FEBRUARY 2011

February 3, 2011

Hi Holly,

Just to update you that prayers are needed for Mom who now has problems with loss of appetite, possibly due to the new med she is on after her stent procedure. Please pray that she regains her appetite and that the doctor can help with treating this side

MOM'S LAST DAYS

effect with a safe and effective medicine. Also prayers for her skin ailment which has flared up due to not having her routine doses of steroids which was necessary in order for her foot problem to resolve.

Also prayers for IMPD policeman David Moore's repose. His family is now in the process of donating his organs after he suffered gunshot wounds.

Prayers also for the Dale Moog, who's death anniversary was this past week. God rest his soul.

Prayers for good weather next week for safe travel to Indy for dr appt.

Prayers for safety of the US and Egyptian citizens who are caught in the violence, and for an end to the violence in the region.

Thanks so much and God bless!

Mary

MOM'S LAST DAYS

February 5, 2011

Hi Baby,

Brida's no is ----.

We can't come today. Mom is not feeling well.

Take care,

Mary

February 9, 2011

Hello dear Ladies,

Just an update: Surgeon is of the opinion that Mom's back pain is not bec of gallstones but of her compressed vertebra.

He said her bile duct was open and she was making new bile. Her labs were normal. So he said he will recommend she go to an orthopedic med and get physical therapy. Thank you so much for your prayers!

In Jesus and Mary,

Mary

February 9, 2011

Hi Janine,
Mom has had this problem before and physical therapy was effective. In fact she has been asymptomatic for years until now. So we have hopes that another PT treatment will help her once again.
Have a safe trip and thank you for continued prayers.
Mary

MOM'S LAST DAYS

February 9, 2011

Hello dear Ladies,

Just an update: Surgeon is of the opinion that Mom's back pain is not bec of gallstones but of her compressed vertebra. He said her bile duct was open and she was making new bile. Her labs were normal. So he said he will recommend she go to an orthopedic med and get physical therapy. Thank you so much for your prayers!

In Jesus and Mary,

Mary

February 9, 2011

Dear Rheeda,
We just got home. Mom is getting some z's on the couch and Dad and I are in various stages of decompression. The surgeon had

asked me to describe Mom's pain and he thought, after hearing my impressions, that this was consistent with her vertebral problem. He described that her duct (guess that is the opening of her gall bl) was open and was making new bile. So he concluded this was more her bone issue not the stones. He said her liver fcn was normal.

My mission tomorrow is to talk to her PCP and get her to see Mom before the week is out. Mom is on new pain meds, so let's pray she will respond to them w/o having ill effects.

Mom had this back problem years ago, and a few visits to PT did her a lot of good. I'm just glad Mom is not having surgery bec she would have had to stop her Plavix and the surgeon said that doing this would clot her stents so not a good option.

I hope and pray that Mom will be able to have pain relief.

Thank you for your prayers. They did and

MOM'S LAST DAYS

are doing good!

Love,
Mary

February 9, 2011

Hello Ann,

It seems Mom doesn't get her gallbladder taken out. The surgeon told me that her bile ducts was open and bile was flowing freely. He thought that her back pain was bec of a compression of her vertebrae and that she just needs togo to an orthopedic md and get physical therapy. They are giving her a rx for pain meds, then we can all go home.

Thank you so much for your prayers, Ann.

Love,

Mary

February 9, 2011

Hello Ann,

MARY FADERAN

Just got back from having lunch at
home. Mom seemed to be pain free this
afternoon. She had not yet taken her pain
meds. She said it hurt only if she
moved. I think that is an improvement. I
am hoping that she will continue to get
better. Dad said that she ate 2/3rd of a roll
for breakfast and a little bit of coffee. She
seems definite about when she wants to eat
and drink. I did persuade her last night to
drink a little more fluids as her HIDA scan
had given her this radioactive stuff,
something that is supposed to help the MD
figure out her gall bladder on the
screen. The website on this scan said that
the radioactivity is not very much, and yet
they suggested that the patient drink a lot
of fluids to flush it out.   Yes, I have
been under a lot of stress
lately. Besides my Mom's health issues,
my project was due out this week. God is
good, and I was able to accomplish
the deadline in good time. Today at our
prayer meeting at work, our CEO prayed
not only for my Mom but for me. I was
very touched and wanted to cry. In fact,

MOM'S LAST DAYS

one of us, the Global Manager, Denny, had reached for a tissue at the end of the meeting. Our company is just great this way, how everyone does pray for each other and gives encouragement to each other. I'm so glad to have these people as my superiors.   Well, this weekend I am going to pick up Mom's wig. I have delayed going there due to Mom's illness and the woman at the wig store has been very understanding. But, of course, there is no other way but to get the wig tomorrow. I think Mom will be ok wearing without trying it on first. Other than that, I don't have a lot of things to do, unless I go to my gym and spend a little time on the treadmill. I'll see how it goes. I know that Dad probably needs to go out for a while just to take a breather. He has been staying home with Mom all week and I'm sure he's also stressed out. But, really Mom is not someone who's totally helpless, but she does need to be watched so that if she needs to get out of bed or get up to stand, someone will help. I'm worried that her

MARY FADERAN

lack of appetite is just running her batteries down, though. I've yet to hear from the Dr's office. Maybe they will call home instead of call me. Guess that is all for now. I do hope that you have a good weekend. Thank you again for your prayers. They are being felt. Love and prayers, Mary

February 09, 2011

Hello Ann,

It seems Mom doesn't get her gallbladder. gallbladder taken out. The surgeon told me that her bile ducts was open and bile was flowing freely. He thought that her back pain was bec of a compression of her vertebrae and that she just needs to go to an orthopedic md and get physical therapy. They are giving her a rx for pain meds, then we can all go home.

Thank you so much for your prayers, Ann.

MOM'S LAST DAYS

Love,

Mary

February 10, 2011

Hi Ann,

it was good to get back home with Mom yesterday. She is on new pain meds and seems to be in less pain esp at rest. She still doesn't eat much. Only jello and 7 Up. I spoke to her Dr's nurse today. They are going to see about PT. They were supposed to call me back this afternoon but didn't.

I hope by this weekend Mom will be feeling better. Now I am beginning to feel the exhaustion set in.

Thanks again for your prayers.

Much love,

Mary

MOM'S LAST DAYS

February 11, 2011

Hello Ann,

Just got back from having lunch at home. Mom seemed to be pain free this afternoon. She had not yet taken her pain meds. She said it hurt only if she moved. I think that is an improvement. I am hoping that she will continue to get better. Dad said that she ate 2/3rd of a roll for breakfast and a little bit of coffee.

She seems definite about when she wants to eat and drink. I did persuade her last night to drink a little more fluids as her HIDA scan had given her this radioactive stuff, something that is supposed to help the MD figure out her gall bladder on the screen. The website on this scan said that the radioactivity is not very much, and yet they suggested that the patient drink a lot of fluids to flush it out.

Yes, I have been under a lot of stress lately. Besides my Mom's health issues, my project was due out this week. God is good, and I was able to accomplish the deadline in good time. Today at our prayer meeting at work, our CEO prayed not only for my Mom but for me. I was very touched and wanted to cry. In fact, one of us, the Global Manager, Denny, had reached for a tissue at the end of the meeting. Our company is just great this way, how everyone does pray for each other and gives encouragement to each other. I'm so glad to have these people as my superiors.

Well, this weekend I am going to pick up Mom's wig. I have delayed going there due to Mom's illness and the woman at the wig store has been very understanding. But, of course, there is no other way but to get the wig tomorrow. I think Mom will be ok wearing without trying it on first. Other than that, I don't have a lot of things to do, unless I go to my gym and spend a little time on the treadmill. I'll see how it goes. I know that Dad probably needs to go out for a while just to take a breather. He has been staying home with Mom all week and

MOM'S LAST DAYS

I'm sure he's also stressed out. But, really Mom is not someone who's totally helpless, but she does need to be watched so that if she needs to get out of bed or get up to stand, someone will help. I'm worried that her lack of appetite is just running her batteries down, though.

I've yet to hear from the Dr's office. Maybe they will call home instead of call me.

Guess that is all for now. I do hope that you have a good weekend. Thank you again for your prayers.

They are being felt.

Love and prayers,

Mary

February 13, 2011

Hi Julia,

MARY FADERAN

Just another update.

Mom is on pain meds and she gets pain when she moves. She is also weakened due to her lack of appetite and eating very little. She does eat when she has to take her meds, but it is only a little of food, a half bottle of Boost, half a roll of bread and a little bit of coffee. Sometimes she has jello with some fruit but that is only half of the cup. She tells me of
her beautiful dreams about St Padre Pio or the Blessed Mother.

I will be away from the computer most of tomorrow since we will be taking Mom to see her Dermatologist in
Indianapolis. However, this might change if Mom is not strong enough to get
ready or to travel. This is an hour long trip. She says she has a strong desire to go there. I do have my cell phone that can receive my yahoo mail.

Mary

MOM'S LAST DAYS

February 13, 2011

She does have some kidney problems. I spoke to the pharmacist just a few mins ago and she said that Bonine orDramamine should work. She-Mom-doesn't drink a lot of water either.

MARY FADERAN

February 13, 2011

I am now. I had to go out for a SFO mtg
but came home and got her to drink water
three x in an hour and some OJ.

She fights me some so I let her drowse but
not before getting her to promise another
sip or two in a half hour. This is

chronic with her, tho and her dr has
already told her to drink more.

February 13, 2011

Dear Father,

Please pray for my Mom, Sally. She has a
bad back, and has had loss of appetite from
her new med-Plavix. She eats very little
plus gets nausea grom her pain meds. She
is also having a flareup of her skin ailment.

MOM'S LAST DAYS

She is going to see her doctors tomorrow, Tue and Wed for her different ailments.

Thank you, Fr Cajetan.

February 13, 2011

Hi Holly,

Just an update: Mom is still having pain in her back, but is on pain meds and the pain occurrs [sic] only when she is moving. She has a few Dr's appts this coming week. She has gotten weak due to having no appetite and sometime nausea. I think this is due to the new med (Plavix) that she is on. Please continue your prayers for recovery and healing.

Thanks again,

Mary

February 13, 2011

Hello Ann,

I'm almost done for the day as I've got to see Dr B this pm. I've sent my boss something to read and hope that he will be ok with it.

Mom did not do too well with that new med to help her appetite. It was a drug that is called mirtazapine (Remeron) and is really for those who have major depression, but its side effects include weight gain and increased appetite. My Mom fell asleep pronto once she took it and she slept for a day and is still feeling the effects. She also had a bad nightmare and now is having a back pain. These are also side effects of this drug. I'm not sure if her doctor is able to help her since Mom is pretty much susceptible to these meds

MOM'S LAST DAYS

because she is so sensitive. I did call her Dr's nurse today and told them about this and that Mom is not taking the med anymore after the first dose. I don't know what those people in the drs' office are now thinking. Feel like they are not able to do much about this.

In the meantime, the weather was pretty awful Tuesday and I went home early. The sleet was just coming down buckets. Monday evening I had to run to Walmart to get a couple of items to cook something for supper. Well, the parking lot was just crazy, everyone and every car seemed to be either going in or coming out. I got home about an hour later, but it was ghastly. Then Wed our company closed the doors for the day and I stayed home. There was a lot of snow, but not as much as they predicted. About 6 inches, although there was some drifting. And, the snow was crusty and hard to shovel, from what I hear. The people that came to shovel our drive only did the drive and not the walkway to our front door. I guess that was enough for now. Maybe they will do

it sometime, but I am not really sure. I
could call and ask, but I won't push my
luck:-) last night I made this angel hair
pasta with diced tomatoes and basil. Mom
seemed to like that. She just does not want
to eat anything. And she's really feeling
upset at how we can't go to Indy to see her
dr (bec of the weather) to get him to give
her the shot she needs to help her skin
ailment. But, we made another appt to see
him Tuesday. I am crossing my fingers,
praying for good weather that day.

I am feeling like maybe stressed out too,
esp last Tuesday with this weather. I also
noticed that I felt this pain in my chest but
I believe that is an after effect of the
ativan. That med is bad news to me now
that I'm off it. I took one half pill this past
weekend and then this appeared. It
does this after I don't take it regularly. Bad
stuff. Don't take it, Ann.

I do hope that your BP will be better
soon. Did they take you off the statin bec

MOM'S LAST DAYS

you were already at a normal cholesterol? Why not give you a BP med instead?

Glad that your grandson is staying over. Children are just precious. My cousin Joanne who had a baby in september has baby pictures on FB and little Chloe is growing fast and her smile is so adorable. I am sure that her parents are just so much in love with her. I know that Chloe gives me Mom a smile. That is so good for Mom now. She's needing a little encouragement and a lift.

Well, I best get going and tidy up before I head out to see Dr B.

Hope you have a wonderful weekend!

love and prayers,

Mary

MARY FADERAN

February 13, 2011

Hi Rheeda,

I saw your email to Mom. She tried to write you back but fell asleep. She has been drowsy most of the day as she is on pain meds. We hope her visits to her drs next will give her a way to find healing and relief. I think that she is going to get physical therapy for her back. Her loss of appetite is still a problem, tho. It is a side effect of her medicine that was given to keep her stents from clotting up. I am trying to get her to drink more water.

Will keep you updated when there's news.

Love,

Mary

MOM'S LAST DAYS

February 14, 2011

Hi Fr Stan,

Please continue to pray for my Mom, Sally. She is suffering from a compression fracture of her T11 vertebra and loss of appetite. She is taking pain meds, a piece of bread some sips of coffee in the a.m., a little Boost a couple of times and maybe if she has to a few sips of water or a little jello. She sees three Drs today, tomorrow and wedesday [sic].

Thank you and God bless!

Mary

February 14, 2011

Holly,

How did your parents' PCP deal with the N&V?

Mary

February 14, 2011

Sorry - nausea and vomiting :-(

February 14, 2011

Primary care physician

February 14, 2011

It might be good to know so that I can tell Mom's dr tomorrow when we go.

MOM'S LAST DAYS

Thanks,

Mary

MARY FADERAN

February 15, 2011

Central. If possible could you give her a blessing and anointing? It was good for her the previous time you did that.

Thank you,

Mary

February 15, 2011

They are moving her to East. They are concerned that she may have cancer somewhere. We are very concerned.

February 15, 2011

MOM'S LAST DAYS

Thanks, Glenda. She has gotten checked at the hospital.

MARY FADERAN

February 15, 2011

I don't know for sure, but another couple of days, siguro *[maybe]*.

February 15, 2011

Julia,

Mom is back in the hospital. Her kidneys have shut down. They also found her calcium levels are high and they are saying they are concerned about cancer. This is very scary news. So they aren't sure yet and they say it could be due to her renal failure too. Please send more prayers to St Pio.

I will keep you posted.

Mary

MOM'S LAST DAYS

February 15, 2011

She's in ER again. Dr said her labs were abnormal. Specifically her kidney fcn. No idea but she might be here for a day or so. Giving her fluids.

Mary

February 16, 2011

Dear Father,

Mom's drs came to visit. They will be checking her parathyroid gland status, and also perform a colonoscopy when her kidneys are working better. Possibly on Friday. I had a good chat with Dr Shinn. He was nice to show me Mom's labs on the computer. She has got a high calcium level, which is quite unusual. I did note that her last calcium level was less so that is encouraging.

MOM'S LAST DAYS

They will also start Mom on Lovenox to keep her from getting a clot.

I am grateful for the good people who are working to help my Mom. God is good indeed, and He surely lives in St E hospital's staff.

Perhaps my Mom will be able to receive Holy Communion soon? She is still nauseous but perhaps in the next day or so she will improve there too.

Our best regards to you, Father Cajetan,

Mary

February 16, 2011

Hi Glenda,

St Elizabeth East. She's pretty much out of it and has asked me to tell others that she

MARY FADERAN

would prefer not to have visitors until she
feels more like herself. I will tell her that
you are praying for her.

Mary

MOM'S LAST DAYS

February 16, 2011

Hello Everyone,

Just an update. I spoke to Dad just a few minutes ago. The doctor came to let them know that Mom is going to have a colonoscopy on Friday. Mom's CT scan last Monday showed some inflammation of her bowel and they are concerned that this is a possible reason for the elevation of her calcium levels. I asked Dad if Mom had eaten today and he said no, that she did not like to eat what they brought - soup and apple juice. She has not thrown up since this morning, though. Again, please keep up your prayers. She's still on iv fluids. I will send you another update later when we have spent more time at the hospital. Oh, by the way, there was a "swallow" test she went through this morning and she passed that one. The technician who did the test made her do different exercises to test how her muscles that controll [sic] her swallowing reflexes were doing. The technician said that she will do this again two days in a row, and then conclude her testing with a report.

Dad and I are ok. Have been subsisting on fast food and hospital food. I'm getting to know a lot about the geography of the new hospital with regards to where the vending machines are etc.

Oh and also, Fr Cajetan (chaplain) came by to say hello to Mom and to give her a blessing and anointing. He also sprinkled holy water over us. Mom was very happy about Father's visit.

Have a good day and God bless all of us.

Mary

PS Please let the other members of the Rosary group know - I don't have their email addresses.

February 16, 2011

MOM'S LAST DAYS

Hi Rheeda,

Yes, I had to go to work. Actually, my boss has been allowing me the time to go and take Mom to the different docs she sees, and to take her to Urgent Care and take her to ER visits. He does understand that Mom is first when it comes to family and life. He also has 80-year old parents. But, I am the only one he can rely on for the work we do. Like today I came in and found out that he did not approve something that was actually ok to approve because he had forgotten that we had an approval for it. It is a grind to work. Dad is with Mom when I am here (and I did stay with Mom early today for acouple [sic] of hours) and Mom knows that I have responsibilities to keep abreast of what is going on at work. When she will have her colonoscopy onFriday [sic] I plan to be there when she goes and when they bring her back and after. Since Mom is basically sleeping most of the time, focusing on her wellbeing is a little hard since I cannot do more than watch and sit with her. I know that she would like to have me with her all the time. It is a difficult thing to know what to do. I hope you forgive me that I cannot be with Mom all of the time.

Mary

MOM'S LAST DAYS

February 16, 2011

Hi Glenda,

Thanks for your prayers. They are being felt. I don't really have any idea what we need right now. I wish I could be here all the time, but I had to work today. One of my cousins was critical of my not being with Mom and focus on her getting well. That was not good to hear. Mom was not awake most of the day and Dad was with her even if I wasn't.

Plus I knew the drs were not around till after 5, so trying to wait for them to show up would be futile. So kainis. Well, I've vented. Thanks for the sympathetic shoulder. I think if the colonoscopy is still on for Friday I could take the day off.

Mary

MARY FADERAN

February 17, 2011

Hi Father Stan,

Mom is now in the hospital. She was so dehydrated, her labs were out of whack. She is on IV fluids, and is not able to take drink or food due to her nausea/vomiting. They are concerned that she has high calcium levels in her blood, which they think is pointing to a cancer in her system, possibly in her colon. They are also going to see if she has a parathyroid disease, which also causes this high calcium. Tomorrow afternoon she will have a colonoscopy procedure. I hope and pray that they won't find anything there. They did a CT scan last week and saw gallstones and also 'thickening' of the intestine in the sigmoid colon. Then, the ER doctor asked if she had irritable bowel disease. Did not mention anything like

MOM'S LAST DAYS

cancer. They did labs on her then, too, and said it seemed to be normal, though I don't know what exactly they looked at if they looked at calcium also. It's very troublesome. But I am confident that God is taking care of everything, and the hospital staff are good and are doing their best.

Thank you Father, for your prayers and blessing.

Mary

February 17, 2011

Hi Julia,

My Mom is getting better they say as far as her kidney fcn. They still plan on the colonoscopy tomorrow. They say her CEA level is high, something that is a protein seen in patients who have cancer. This has stunned us. However the dr says not everyone with a high CEA has cancer. So we are feeling scared. I asked the dr what if they don't find cancer in the colon and he said they will look for it somewhere else. It is pretty rough on us. I am with Mom in her room. We look towards tomorrow feeling scared but hopeful.

Mary

February 17, 2011

Dear Sr Ann,

Thank you so much for your email and good thoughts and prayers. Mom smiled after hearing your words. She is surely gaining many graces from the prayers and sacrifices sent to God for her healing. I spent the night in her room and got acquainted with her night nurses. She still

MOM'S LAST DAYS

is not taking food. I hope today we will turn a corner. I will keep you updated.

Yours in Christ and Mary,

Mary

February 18, 2011

Hi Everyone,

The gi dr couldn't do the exam this afternoon since Mom still had a lot of stool in her rectum. The nurse only did one enema and she should have done 2 but they wanted to get Mom sooner etc. Dr will prep Mom over the wkend. They will try again Monday. Please continue your prayers.

God bless us all!

Mary

February 18, 2011

Glenda,

Na-delay ang col-scope *[the colonoscopy was delayed]*. Dami pa daw stool, hindi

MOM'S LAST DAYS

lahat na alis *[there was so much stool, not all were removed]*. Monday gagawin *[will be performed Monday]*. Dr will "prep" her over the next 2 days.

I will let you know whenever.

Mary

February 18, 2011

Hi Holly,

They will do the colonoscopy on Mom this afternoon, around 3 or so. She is much more animated in her behavior - just basically due to having had an infusion of 5% dextrose-saline. Doh. They could have done that a little sooner.

The other concern is, while her Ca level is now normal and everything is normal about her eletrolytes [sic], her CEA test result came back high. Have you heard of this one? It is a marker that is seen in patients who have cancer, but, this CEA cannot be a predictor of a person's state of having cancer. Ie [sic]. you can't just test everyone for CEA since not everyone who has it has cancer. I think that is a little confusing. I checked Google for some info and they say that CEA levels are monitored for cancer patients who have undergone Chemo/Rad to see if these have been successful. Anyway I know that God is in charge, and His Will be done in everything.

She still has nausea/vomiting - even when she has to take some of her meds. It's a little like the lottery, sometimes she doesn't throw up after taking pills, other times, she does.

Thanks again, Holly, for the prayers.

Mary

February 18, 2011

I asked her dr the question "If you don't find cancer in her colon, what are you

MOM'S LAST DAYS

going to do?" to which he replied that they will look elsewhere for the cancer.

February 19, 2011

She had a couple of enemas. But she has been pooping every 15 min, so it has been a bit of a night so far.

MARY FADERAN

February 19, 2011

Hi Rheeda,
Mom's been on the bedpan on and off for the past 14 hrs. They will prep her (cleanse) over these 2 days. It has been miserable for her to not be able to sleep. I've been awake most of the night. When the nurses aren't able to respond to her bell I have stepped in to get her cleaned up. Her poor bottom is getting sore.

I hope that things get more manageable today.

Hope you have a good weekend.

I will let you know the latest.

Mary

MOM'S LAST DAYS

February 19, 2011

Dear Eileen,
I'm undergoing tests for my entire system to be good but Monday it will be a colonscopy ti see whether cancer elements lurk somewhere. Am in the drinking stage of this gallon of Nulytely and I'm blurry-eyed and cery weak but I thought about you and to please inform Winnie, Erwin and Erving. Pls call Sis. Teresita Castrillo for her prayers. She has no email. Also Angelyn, Thank you to all of you and God love you all. Love,Tita

February 19, 2011

Hello Cuz,
We three are quietly reading, sleeping or emailing this evening. Mom had to drink this beverage to clean her intestines. Half a gallon today and the other half tomorrow. Her labs are mostly good. Her kidney dr gave her some meds for the ones that were

a bit low. The scope is scheduled for
Monday 12:30 pm.

It is at least a quieter day than last night.
Tonight I stay over. I already heard Mass
today. Dad will go tomorrow a.m.

Well, other than this we are doing ok.
Mom is only allowed liquids. She is just
having decaf and a popsicle.

Good night and God bless,
Mary

February 19, 2011

Hi Rheeda,

Mom's been on the bedpan on and off for
the past 14 hrs. They will prep her
(cleanse) over these 2 days. It has been

miserable for her to not be able to sleep.
I've been awake most of the night. When
the nurses aren't able to respond to her bell
I have stepped in to get her cleaned up. Her

MOM'S LAST DAYS

poor bottom is getting sore.

I hope that things get more manageable today.

Hope you have a good weekend.

I will let you know the latest.

Mary

February 20, 2011

Hi Ann,

it was good to get back home with Mom yesterday. She is on new pain meds and seems to be in less pain esp at rest. She still doesn't eat much. Only jello and 7 Up. I spoke to her Dr's nurse today. They are going to see about PT.

They were supposed to call me back this afternoon but didn't.

I hope by this weekend Mom will be

feeling better. Now I am beginning to feel the exhaustion set in.

Thanks again for your prayers.

Much love,

Mary

February 21, 2011

Hello Dear Ones,

Praise God Mom's colonoscopy went well and the dr gave her good marks. She has a mild diverticulosis and internal hemmorhoids. Thank you so much for all your prayers. We are so grateful to God for taking good care of my Mom.

God bless us everyone!

Love,

MOM'S LAST DAYS

Mary and Dad

February 21, 2011

Hi Annette,

She is currently sleeping off the sedative. I think once they start her on her food and see that she is ok and able to

walk around they might let her come home with us in a couple of days.

Thanks again for the wonderful prayers. I think she may have some posts on FB pretty soon!

Love,

Mary

February 21, 2011

Hi Marilu,

MARY FADERAN

I think perhaps when Mom is back home
and in better surroundings and disposition,
we will surely be happy to see you:-)

I don't know when she is
getting discharged. I think Mom should be
ready sometime within the next few days.

Mary

February 21, 2011

Hello Everyone,

Mom's colonoscopy is at noon today. Thanks
for your prayers.

Mary

MOM'S LAST DAYS

February 21, 2011

Hi Marilu,

Mom has a reply for your email:

Hi Malu! Appreciate your prayers. Purpose is to check for gallstones (?), kidney problem (cuz I lost weight fr[sic] size 8 to 4 ptite [sic]) or colon problem since I became irregular then there's my heart and bLood prssure [sic] which is mOnitored [sic]) so all the red zones better be kind to me. I trust in God and Mary your kind prayers. God bless you!

Sally

February 21, 2011

Hi Holly,

We took Mom to the ER. She has been vomiting three x today and yesterday and Friday. The pain in her side has been there for days.

They have taken labs etc.

Will keep y

February 21, 2011

Dear Rosemary,

Yes, she is eating now. I left her this afternoon eating her angel cake with strawberry topping:-)

Thanks so much, Rosemary, we are very grateful.

Mary

February 21, 2011

Hi Rheeda,

MOM'S LAST DAYS

I don't think they did any removing of anything. The doctor said there was nothing to do, just said he is off her case unless the attending will ask him to. I think Mom's diverticulosis is so mild that it has not affected her - she loves to eat nuts and there was no painful after effects.

Thank you again, Rheeda, for your prayers. We are truly grateful.

Mary

February 21, 2011

Hi Holly,

I'm glad to tell you that Mom's colonoscopy went well. She has a mild diverticulosis (not painful at all), and internal hemorrhoids in her sigmoid colon. The Dr said he was off the case now unless the attending asks him to.

Thanks so much for the prayers. I hope and pray that she gets back to her activities and embraces the new changes for her diet and care.

Mary

February 21, 2011

You know, you are so right! My Mom IS an angel and it was just great that she chose angel cake to eat for dessert. She surely does deserve such sweet rewards for having gone through so much stress, pain, humiliation and trial! I also am glad to tell you that she has been speaking with anyone she meets about God and His Saints. So, I think that while Mom is receiving good healthcare at St E, she is also giving back to its staff a bit of her wisdom and love for God.

Mary

MOM'S LAST DAYS

February 21, 2011

Yes, she was discharged this evening. We thought it was a bit sudden but the nurse said that since her scope was good they thought there was no reason to keep her longer.

She is quite weak still, barely able to stand. But she ate lunch and dinner and took her meds. It may be a few days before she can feel strong enough to get back into her regular activities. Plus her foot is still causing her pain.

She did get pain meds so they are helping.

Thank you, Carole, for your prayers.

Love,

Mary

MARY FADERAN

February 22, 2011

Hello Ann,

I am glad to tell you Mom is back home. Her colonoscopy yesterday showed no problems (she has mild

diverticulosis, and internal hemorrhoids [sic]). We thought she might stay a day longer but Dad called me at work to tell me she was being released yesterday. So I went home to get some clothes for her and got back to the hospital. She is still a bit weak. Yesterday she was so weary, slept for most of the evening after eating a meal. This morning I got her up to go to the bathroom and gave her her eye drops.

Yes, it has been such an ordeal. I was waiting in the waiting room when they were doing the 'scope and praying. Dad and I were there, prayed the rosary with Mom before she was wheeled out and prayed the Divine Mercy when she was there. They got finished within 1/2 hr of her getting wheeled out. The doctor

MOM'S LAST DAYS

showed us pictures of her bowel.

She is still prone to vomit, so it is a little tricky to get her to eat or take her meds. They treated her with i.v. meds for the vomiting, and then at home I obtained these dissolvable tablets to place on the tongue. She had croissant for breakfast which got vomited, I got home and she took some of last night dinner for lunch. She took her morning meds and settled down to rest.

I called her Dr to report this also. They are faxing an order for her PT to start. I hope that this won't be too much for Mom. But she does have the back pain and if the PT helped before it should do this again.

She likes the St E PT people.

If you go on FB, you can see Mom's entries.

It was so good to sleep in my own bed last night. I woke up still feeling like I could sleep another hour or two.

Dr B called me today and asked how Mom was. I had called him last week and left a message. I will see Dr B on Thursday this week.

They cut out her Lasix and Benicar. Dr Shinn, the nephrologist, said that Lasix is hard on the kidneys.

And then her dosage on the coreg got cut in half. I don't know what her BP is at this time. She tended to be slightly high in the hospital. They also noted that she was getting atrial fib from time to time, mostly

when she was vomiting because she was just so exhausted by it.

They also cut out her calcium supplements. They thought that she was overmedicated with calcium. So only her multivitamins.

At least she doesn't have a lot of meds to take, maybe that was also causing stress to her system. Dr Shinn is quite good. He explained to Mom about making sure she is drinking fluids. Now I think she understands.

MOM'S LAST DAYS

Well, today after work I will go and get her some healthy snacks, and also some food to make for dinner.

Thanks so much for the prayers, Ann. Mom needs to recover from this trip to St E, for sure. I really think that 2 trips to St E hospital in 2 months is plenty!

Love,

Mary

February 23, 2011

Hi Eileen,

Thank you so much for your prayers. We were very concerned about the colonoscopy results, and every prayer helped. Mom is home now since Monday evening. She's working on getting back her strenght [sic] and her appetite.

I hope you are well and the family is also doing well. We'll try to give you a call this weekend, ok?

Love,

Agnes

February 27, 2011

I have heard of celiac disease. Will ask the dr about this.

Dad and I are more able to deal with this knowing that the drs are watching her. It was harder for us to see how much Mom suffered at home unable to eat without vomiting plus the pain in her side.

Thank you for your prayers!

Mary

MOM'S LAST DAYS

February 27, 2011

Hello All,

We took Mom to the ER again as she has not eaten/drank today and her side is painful. I talked to the dr on call and he suggested this ER visit. she vomits at the mention of food.

The dr in ER was just here. They will have some tests done on her and give her fluids.

I will keep you posted.

Mary

February 27, 2011

Carole,

The nurse just came to tell us that the ER dr and Dr Welch (Mom's dr) spoke and they are trying to determine whether Mom is going to Methodist hosp [sic] or stay in St E. Dr W is concerned that Mom needs a higher level of care bec she has now been to st [sic] E twice for the same thing and has not been resolved.

We are concerned about the Methodist option. It is a distance from here and we don't know how it is going to work.

Prayers definitely needed.

Mary

February 28, 2011

Hi Carole,

Mom has been able to have orange juice this a.m. She also went for an MRI this afternoon, and then a gall bladder specialist is going to see her too.

I am on my way to drop by my home and will be going to the hospital with my Dad who will pick me up. I hope to have more details later.

Thanks again for your prayers. We are

MOM'S LAST DAYS

blessed indeed to have our Schoenstatt friends!

Mary

February 28, 2011

Hi Folks,

Mom is being admitted to the Observation ward. The nurse mentioned that the GI consult is planned. We are glad that they decided not to transfer Mom to Methodist in Indy. That would have been more stress for all of us, with Mom so far and Dad and me commuting.

The nurse said she has a room already and is calling report.

Mary

February 28, 2011

MARY FADERAN

Dear Sr Ann,

Yes, we too were glad about her colonoscopy results.

I did get to talk to Mom's nurse this morning and she said that Mom had orange juice this morning. She also said that her blood sugar came back to normal (it was very low last night). They are transferring her (or have already done this) to a regular room (she was in Observation). The GI doctor will take a look at her today. I am not sure when she will be allowed to come home with us. I surely hope that they are going to figure out what has been causing her to have nausea and vomiting [sic]. It seems to me since they told us last night that her liver enzymes were elevated, that she may have had too much of Tylenol which could cause the same symptoms and also make her liver enzymes go up.

Thank you Sr Ann for your prayers and for your support. It has been such a difficult year so far for my Mom and for me and

MOM'S LAST DAYS

Dad as well. Mom had become nauseated/vomiting for about 4 days since she got back home last Monday. She seemed to have had a developing pain on her side (right) and so when she had all those symptoms I thought maybe her gall bladder was having a problem. But, the doctor in the ER said that the ULtrasound [sic] did not show that the gall bladder was inflamed and he focused more on her liver. Very difficult. Then Mom's regular doctor (who was consulted) had considered having Mom transferred to Methodist. So everyone in the family was pretty concerned as it meant that we would be traveling to and from Indy to be with Mom and to attend to her. Fortunately she was admitted to St E.

I also had requested that Mom receive Holy Communion from Blessed SACrament's [sic] EMOHC, and so a nicelady came yesterday after Mass to give MOm [sic] the Eucharist. Fortunately, Mom was able to consume Jesus' Body.

Thanks again, Sr Ann. I will surely keep

you posted.

Mary

February 28, 2011

Hi Annette,

Thanks for your email. Yes, it has been very stressful for all three of us, especially Mom. She's been poked and stuck and pushed and shoved every which way. Plus she's been throwing up and been unable to eat for several days. I just wish that the hospital did not release her last Monday and kept her for at least a day to see if she could really eat and keep her food down.

I spoke to Dad earlier and they said they are going to do an MRI on her upper body today. And then the gall bladder specialist is visiting today too. I just pray that they

MOM'S LAST DAYS

will be able to pinpoint the source of my Mom's problem.

She did get some orange juice to drink this morning. But apparently that is all they have given her. They have also attached this device to her legs to prevent clotting.

Dad and I got home at 1:30 a.m. this morning. I got up at 6:15, said my prayers, then awoke Dad too. He is there with Mom now and I will join them after a bit. I've had two meetings that I attended at work today and tried to focus. I wish I could go to sleep for a few hours and maybe when I get up I'd feel so much more able to do things.

Guess that is all the news at this time. Have a good day - just keep your prayers going.

Love,

Mary

February 28, 2011

Hi Carole,

Mom has been able to have orange juice this a.m. She also went for an MRI this afternoon, and then a gall bladder specialist is going to see her too.

I am on my way to drop by my home and will be going to the hospital with my Dad who will pick me up. I hope to have more details later.

Thanks again for your prayers. We are blessed indeed to have our Schoenstatt friends!

Mary

February 28, 2011

Hi Folks,

MOM'S LAST DAYS

Mom is being admitted to the Observation ward. The nurse mentioned that the GI consult is planned. We are glad that they decided not to transfer Mom to Methodist in Indy. That would have been more stress for all of us, with Mom so far and Dad and me commuting.

The nurse said she has a room already and is calling report.

Mary

MARY FADERAN

February 28, 2011

Hi Annette,

Thanks for your email. Yes, it has been very stressful for all three of us, especially Mom. She's been poked

and stuck and pushed and shoved every which way. Plus she's been throwing up and been unable to eat for several days. I just wish that the hospital did not release her last Monday and kept her for at least a day to see if she could really eat and keep her food down.

I spoke to Dad earlier and they said they are going to do an MRI on her upper body today. And then the gall bladder specialist is visiting today too. I just pray that they will be able to pinpoint the source of my Mom's problem.

She did get some orange juice to drink this morning. But apparently that is all they

MOM'S LAST DAYS

have given her. They have also attached this device to her legs to prevent clotting.

Dad and I got home at 1:30 a.m. this morning. I got up at 6:15, said my prayers, then awoke Dad too. He is there with Mom now and I will join them after a bit. I've had two meetings that I attended at work today and tried to focus. I wish I could go to sleep for a few hours and maybe when I get up I'd feel so much more able to do things.

Guess that is all the news at this time. Have a good day - just keep your prayers going.

Love,

Mary

MARCH 2011

March 1, 2011

Dear Susana,

Thank you very much for your prayers for Mom. She is quite frail and weak because of not having eaten much in the past few days. They have her on IV fluids. Last night they gave her crackers to eat but then she started vomiting early this morning, quite a bit. It took some time to have the doctor's order for anti-nausea medicine.

MOM'S LAST DAYS

The surgeon came to see us this morning and he described the operation to remove Mom's gall bladder. He said her potassium level is a little low and he wants to have it go up a little before he operates on her. He did say he will do the operation tomorrow. I will let you know what time it will be.

So today she will have some food - maybe ensure or something like it - and hopefully not vomit anymore. I have also requested them to give her Holy Communion today, so that is also planned.

Thank you again. God bless you!

Mary

March 1, 2011

Hello,

Mom's surgeon just dropped by to let us

know her surgery is between 10 am to 12 pm.

She seems better this afternoon but has been vomiting most of the day.

Thank you for your continued prayers.

Mary

March 2, 2011

FYI Mom's surgery is at 1 pm today. She had a good night, got up early at 4:30 then went back to sleep. Still snoozing at 7:10 am.
God bless!
Mary

Hello,
Mom's surgeon just dropped by to let us know her surgery is between 10 am to 12 pm.

MOM'S LAST DAYS

She seems better this afternoon but has been vomiting most of the day.

Thank you for your continued prayers.

Mary

MARY FADERAN

March 3, 2011

HI Glenda,

She's ok today - I talked to Dad and she was sitting on the chair, her Indy friends came by to visit. Also, they brought tons of food (talaga naman ang Pinoy *[that's the Filipino way]*) that Dad said would feed an army. So he told me to bring some plates and dinnerware so we can have a picnic in Mom's room today for supper.

I also learned from Dad that she was looking for food to eat - which delighted her nurse. So, keep your fingers crossed that she is getting better and looking towards a good meal and eating it.

Both Mom and I had a long night last night - she had pains from the surgery - they had inflated her belly with CO_2 gas so it distended her belly and kept her up all

MOM'S LAST DAYS

night.

Anyway, I just got a call from Dad that they are going to put in a PICC line so she can get some parenteral nutrition. I don't know why they are doing it so soon, since she expressed an interest in eating. But, maybe they can't wait. She's not eated in almost a week.

Yes, gallstones is common - my Mom's friend Rosemary had them, Malu had them and someone from CBI said she had them.

I'm looking forward to your talk with Perry, by the way. I hope that things go well.

Mary

March 3, 2011

Hi Janine,

MARY FADERAN

By now you've seen my email about the picc line. Mom's nurse was quite concerned that Mom would really be undernourished with the way she wasn't eating all her food. I was told that Mom had pulled out her i.v. and that her skin on her arm had just peeled back. Mom just had to have a more aggressive nourishment to really get better. We will see how the next day or two goes. She wanted solid food today as she didn't like the yogurt and ensure. I asked her what she would rather eat and she replied Filipino beef soup. She settled for cream of chicken which she ate half of. So the nurse asked the dr if Mom could have solid food so that was approved.
I am told they put in picc lines all the time. I think that should be safe. I am praying Mom will tolerate this too. She has had one procedure after another!
Yes I seem to be losing some weight although I eat a hearty hospital meal daily. It is a bit difficult to enjoy eating when you are worrying and nerve wracked. Thank God for our dear friends! Your support is

MOM'S LAST DAYS

invaluable.
I will update as always,
Love,
.
Mary

MARY FADERAN

March 3, 2011

Hello,

Just another update. Mom is adamant that she will eat today. They were going to put in a PICC line so she could get i.v. nutrition but she said no. I spoke to her on the phone and she said that it seemed that they had "abducted" her to the radiology lab. So, no PICC line. I am glad that she resisted, because I think that is a bit invasive and she is already so full of sticks from needles and she just decided one more needle was enough. So please pray that she keeps the food down.

Also please say a prayer for me and Dad because we're pretty exhausted from the nightly vigils and no sleep (for me).

MOM'S LAST DAYS

Thanks so much!

Mary

March 4, 2011

Hi All,

I am in the radiology waiting room as they are placing a PICC line in Mom. She will be getting parenteral nutrition so that she will recover her strength. The dr has recommended that she go for rehab in a long term acute care hospital so they can continue the nutrition and give her physical and occup therapy.

They think Seton Hospital at St E central is where she will go but they also suggested 2 nursing homes in Lafayette Rosewalk or Mulberry. We have not heard a lot about the latter but a friend has been in Rosewalk.

The nursing homes are backup if Seton is full.

Mom had been anxious about the idea of a longer rehab so please continue to pray for her.

MARY FADERAN

God bless, Mary

MOM'S LAST DAYS

March 4, 2011

Seems that Rosewalk is the one. My Franciscan buddy Betty tells me one of our SFO is a resident and that they have Mass there weekly, with daily Holy Communion. Mom's surgeon thinks Mom is getting better although she must have nutrition from the TPN as well as her meals. Her incisions look good. But she had her gb taken out so it needs to heal.

The dr thinks she can transition to Rosewalk Monday. This ecf is close to the St E Central - about 15 min from home. Dr Guttaputty (sp?) thinks Mom may be at Rosewalk for 2 wks. Dr G is her hospitalist. Nice guy.

The other thing is Mom had thrown up today at the Rad lab. Could be due to the anesthetic or that she isn't ready for solid food yet - tho she had hash browns and peaches for brkfst and chix noodle soup for lunch. The dr is aware and he will monitor.

Well that is all for now. Tomorrow is Saturday. I will be going to Mass and Dad will go Sunday. We had Holy Communion today.

MARY FADERAN

The TPN will start tonite.

Love and prayers,

Mary

March 4, 2011

Hello Everyone,

Mom's dr came by while I was getting breakfast. Mom said he was happy with her labs. He also explained how her PICC line is placed, and the science behind it which satisfied my Mom.

It's clear that Drs need to communicate well with their patients to get cooperation.

Nevertheless I will be going to the Rad lab with her for moral support.

MOM'S LAST DAYS

She has ordered breakfast and we look
forward to a good day today, God willing.

God bless!

Mary

March 4, 2011

Mom says she appreciates your concern
and even tho you haven't greeted her yet
she can feel your affection.

Mary

March 4, 2011

She had hash browns and sliced peaches
with coffee for breakfast. Then she
received Holy Communion. The PICC line

is due in half hour to an hour.

You're right it is a present!

Thanks!

Love,

Agnes

March 4, 2011

Nagpunta si Pollyn kanina [*Pollyn went earlier today*]. She said she will cook a meal and bring it sometime.

Still waiting for those radiology guys.

March 4, 2011

MOM'S LAST DAYS

She is in St E East on Creasy next to Unity. Dito lang kami *[we're here]*. Take 52 going towards the mall then go to McCarty turn L then right on Creasy then you'll see Unity Med Ctr on L then after that St E East. Park at the Visitor's area go to 3rd floor go to your right we are room 62 second door on left.

They will give iv nutrition.

I may still be here when you come. I am supposed to be at a teleconference at 1:30 but the engnr gave me the call in number so I can just stay if needed.

Mary

March 4, 2011

Hi Glenda,

MARY FADERAN

She got it. Thank you so much. We will be here.

Mary

March 5, 2011

Hello Dear Ones,
It is just past 7 am. Mom is recovering from her trip to Radiology for her PICC line and also digesting the news of her imminent rehab at Rosewalk. They tried to get her a bed at St E Rehab (too strenuous) and at St E Seton (both at St E) but that didn't go. But Rosewalk was ok. Mom has not been too excited about either this PICC or the rehab. And she has been feeling discomfort. But when they wanted to give her some pain meds she said her throat hurt. This is possibly due to the aftereffects of her being intubated during surgery. So she did not want to swallow a pill. I just asked her whether she was in pain and she said no, but she was tired of lying in bed.

MOM'S LAST DAYS

So one of the CNA's came to turn her.

You are most welcome to visit. She has already had several visitors, including the folks from Indy and her Schoenstatt friend, Marilu. My good friend Glenda visited yesterday. I am sure Rosewalk is open to visitors. But I will make sure.

Give us a call when you are on your way here. My cell no. is ---.

Love,
Mary

March 5, 2011

Today my Mom's surgeon came to visit. He showed her her gallstones. She was impressed. He said her liver enzymes are getting to be normal and her liver biopsy was ok. He reminded her she has her job to get to eat. So far she has only had a small bite of blueberry muffin and a sip of decaf

MARY FADERAN

coffee.

A good friend Pollyn is bringing Filipino food for lunch. Hopefully this will stimulate her appetite. Mom has always been picky about her food. She wanted nilagang baka *[braised beef]* the day after her surgey but they only allowed liquids.

I am concerned that the PICC placement has made her slightly weak due to another invasive procedure. Plus she has developed a sore throat and they gave her a lozenge.

The TPN she gets contains her daily dose of nutrients. I am reminded of my days as an iv room tech when I helped prepare TPNs. At least I can read the ingredients and know exactly what the words mean:-)

I guess that is all. Will update when there's more to tell.

Mary

MOM'S LAST DAYS

March 5, 2011

Mac they did not have room at Seton. Also
Rosewalk and Mulberry are rhe only ones
that take pt on TPN. We know Rosewalk
accepted her. We don't know when she'll
be moved.
We'll see if I can call you tomorrow.
Thanks,
Mary

March 6, 2011

She just got transferred to ccu. She had
chest pains. Keep her in your prayers,
please.

March 6, 2011

Hi Julia,

MARY FADERAN

I realize that you are traveling but I wanted to request more prayers for my Mom. She will need to go to an extended care facility to recuperate. She is weak and frail and has not been eating well. They have started iv nutrition. Please pray that a good ecf will be found and that my Mom will thrive. She has not wanted to eat much. One of her nurses (night) has asked me about her prognosis and if she will need temporary or permanent nursing care. I said as far as I know this is temporary. But I am praying that Mom will turn a corner and get herself back on track.

Thank you again for your continued prayers.

Mary

March 6, 2011

She had chest pains this morning so they

MOM'S LAST DAYS

decided to put her in CCU. She will be assessed by the cardiologist. They gave her blood thinner, and some more meds. Please keep her in your prayers.

Mary

March 6, 2011

The cardiologist came and after interviewing mom he concluded that she has had a heart attack earlier in the past few days and that today's episode was the manifestation. He said he will have her get an echocardiogram and then let her regular cardiologist take over.

They are monitoring her bp etc.

Please continue your prayers.

March 6, 2011

Hello Everyone,

I just wanted to let you know that your prayers have kept my Mom safeguarded. She must have been so stressed that she

MOM'S LAST DAYS

had this heart attack. I am still wondering how the heart attack happened 4 days ago and only showed today! Considering that she wore a heart monitor throughout the last week. I hope her dr can clear this up.

Dad is pulling a sleepover in Mom's room tonight and I am home to get a good night's sleep. I think Dad and I are going to alternate being with Mom during the overnight.

I hope the night brings healing to my Mom.

Love,

Mary

March 6, 2011

Thank you for your prayers. I don't know what their plans for any transfer. As for phone calls just see if you can email the purdue alums ask them to pray for Mom.

She seemed to have problems breathing earlier. I truly think that they could have kept her under closer observation after the picc was placed.

They said her troponin was high.

Mary

March 6, 2011

Yes, she had chest pains this morning. It was very upsetting. I am not totally sure how, what and when. But she was not well after they placed the PICC line. It might have been too much for her to take.

MOM'S LAST DAYS

March 6, 2011

Hi Holly,

This is urgent. She is now pain free but her bp is low. The Dr thinks that she will be given medication to manage although it will be assessed by the cardiologist.

Updates to come.

March 6, 2011

Yes, we are just so stressed! She is getting stable now. Some friends were visiting us today and Mom seems to be encouraged by them. She was able to eat but not a lot. When we ordered her soup she started to belch. Not sure what is causing this.

MARY FADERAN

I have had little sleep this past few days. I hope that with Mom getting expert monitored care that I can go home tonight and finally get some sleep.

I will tour Cumberland Pointe tomorrow to see what the facilities are like. God willing Mom will be able to go there once she is stable.

I hope my Mom will not feel abandoned by my going home. But I think she is going to be ok.

Thank you Ann for your continued prayers.

Mary

March 6, 2011

No not yet. Mac Sison doesn't recommend Rosewalk sabi di nya gusto ang [*he said he*

MOM'S LAST DAYS

doesn't like the] nursing care. We are hoping to get back

from two places. The other option is Mulberry HC but it is far. Pray that we find one that is good and close to home.

Mary

March 6, 2011

Hi Susana,

Thank you, I would love a soup. Vegetable or chicken noodle soup.

My Mom is in 2South room 22.

Love,

Mary

March 6, 2011

Rheeda,

I didn't realze [sic] I missed sending this to you.

Mom is resting now. I am grateful that she has been able to recover. We will see tomorrow how much damage was done to her heart. Her heart rate is stable and her bp is stable. Prayers have averted a worse outcome. God be praised!

March 7, 2011

Dear Fr Stan,

My. Mom needs prayers. She had a heart attack and has had a crisis today and is in heart failure. She is on a bipap machine, her lungs are filling with fluid and they may have to aspirate or even put her on the respirator. Right now she is responding to the bipap. I am entrusting all to God.

Thank you Father and God bless! I will go

MOM'S LAST DAYS

to your website and buy a couple rosaries:-)

In Jesus through Mary,

Mary

March 7, 2011

Hello,

Well, by now you may have heard that Mom had a heart attack. It was not a big one. She is now in CCU,

resting comfortably. I just went to see her over lunch and she had finished eating lunch. Not a lot but at least maybe 1/2 of her chicken noodle soup. She also had a half a cup of coffee. That is a good step in the right direction. She seemed fine, although I noticed she was catching her breath. I looked at her respiration on the monitor and it was a little over the limit but then it went back to normal. I rang for the nurse, although I had already left before the nurse came. Dad had asked me to brimg [sic] Mom's Boost to the hospital as this was what Mom used to drink at home and the doctor had specifically wanted me to bring it. The hospital has Ensure and Mighty Shake but Mom doesn't like Ensure. Not yet sure what Mighty Shake might be like.

Anyway, she can have the Boost.

As far as ECFs, I've not been able to get her into any of the places that I called – Cumberland Pointe, GreenTree (they are private payer and not skilled nursing through Medicare), Westminster and University Place - due to her having TPN. So, the other places are Mulberry and Rosewalk. I've spoken to the social worker and she is putting Mom's info over to Mulberry. One of my friends does not recommend Rosewalk, so I suppose it may have to be Mulberry. Dad thinks it is too far, though. But I told him that Mom must have good nursing care so that she will recover sooner. And if Rosewalk isn't up to

MOM'S LAST DAYS

par, then we will need to consider the other option. The social worker also said that Seton did not accept Mom because she didn't reach their requirements (she needs more than a TPN to be accepted).

That is the latest. Mom also had her ultrasound this a.m. but the cardiologist has not yet appeared. He may come later this afternoon.

Guess that is all, if you have any ideas, please let me know.

Mary

March 7, 2011

Hi Sr Ann,

Yes, she had one, apparently, 4 days before Sunday. They tested her cardiac enzyme (troponin) level yesterday and that is how they figured the timing. She was anxious during the early morning yesterday and they nurse had given her some morphine, and then later on she wanted to get out of bed and onto the chair. It was also clear to me that she was breathing too deeply, like it was hard for her to breathe. Her surgeon came to see her and must have seen her state and ordered the test.

We all were stunned by the news. I am so glad that she is resting now and is comfortable. I don't know, Sr Ann, but I wish her nurses in the regular unit had been more cognizant of this problem, but perhaps because they are understaffed, they don't see it. The only one who mentioned Mom's "decline" was the night nurse Saturday-Sunday. I think that now that Mom is stabilized, her current nurse thinks that all Mom needs to do now is to start eating real food and that is where the problem lies - Mom feels nausea still with food. They thought that the gall bladder surgery would fix that problem but apparently it is still there, although not as bad as before with almost continuous vomiting. It was a terrible time.

Yes, please pray for Mom and I surely hope that she can get over this roadblock in her progress.

Mary

March 7, 2011

Hi Eileen,

Yes I had a good rest last night. I will tell Mom when I see her today.

Love,

Agnes

March 7, 2011

MARY FADERAN

She had a serious crisis this afternoon. She couldn't breathe so they gave her several meds and iv's. They have her on a bipap machine and she is breathing better. The pulmonary dr talked to me and said she is in heart failure, and there is an accumulation of fluid in her lungs and pleural space. The machine is doing a good job. They took a chest xray a few min ago. Hopefully it will show some progress. Her dr is Dr Ahsan. A short guy but has a good bedside manner.

Dad spent the night last night. Both he and I will stay with her tonight.

Our trust is in God.

Love,

Mary

MOM'S LAST DAYS

March 7, 2011

She is resting comfortably now. She took her bp pill also which is good. She did not want to eat. But her iv nutrition is ongoing. The resp therapy lady came to adjust her mask since it seemed not too snug after she took her pill. Her nurse Jonni is a perky blonde who she had the first time she went in to the hospital. We like Jonni.

I hope she will stay stable and get better. Dr Ahsan did mention to Jonni that he did not think Mom needs to be on the respirator so that is good to hear. He seems like he's pretty smart. He thought I was an employee at first when he stared at my slacks and Birkenstocks.

Well, dears, let us rest in God's spirit tonight and look forward to a bright morning.

Mary

MARY FADERAN

MOM'S LAST DAYS

March 7, 2011

Dear Fr Stan,

My. [sic] Mom needs prayers. She had a heart attack and has had a crisis today and is in heart failure. She is on a bipap machine, her lungs are filling with fluid and they may have to aspirate or even put her on the respirator. Right now she is responding to the bipap. I am entrusting all to God.

Thank you Father and God bless! I will go to your website and buy a couple rosaries:-)

In Jesus through Mary,

Mary

March 8, 2011

MARY FADERAN

Dear Jane,

I am so glad you will be praying. I'm really nervous about this. But God's in charge, so I am placing all my trust in His Goodness and Mercy.

Thanks so much,

Mary:-)

March 8, 2011

Hello,

I don't want to scare you but we need to really pray for the next step that the Drs are planning for Mom. She perked up

MOM'S LAST DAYS

today, and looked a bit stronger, able to talk with her dr and her visitors (thanks, Gary and Jenny) this morning. I went to work today with the thought that she was getting better. I got a phone call from Dr Yaacoub, her cardiologist, who told me that he thought Mom was stronger today. He said that he wants to do an angiogram on her in the next couple of days. He said that her ejection fraction before her heart attack was 60% and now it is 20 or 25% (I don't remember the exact number). So he will need to help her and the angiogram is the thing he will do. I don't know how much more she can go through, but Dr Yaacoub has performed this procedure numerous times as well as on Dad. Mom needs to eat a little more food to get her into a stronger constitution. I hope you could just offer prayers and sacrifices of your day for Mom's successful angiogram. She probably cannot go on with only 20% of heart function and expect to do what she does in her daily activities.

Many thanks! God bless!

MARY FADERAN

Mary

Please feel free to forward this to the others that I haven't thought about.

MOM'S LAST DAYS

March 8, 2011

Yes, I will include Winnie. My Yahoo account did not have her email.

I don't know how much this is going to stress her. I know that she was able to tolerate the stent placement for her thigh, but this is going to her heart. I am trusting that God is going to be the hand that will guide her cardiologist. Her cardiologist is a very good doctor, and he listens to God a lot in his work. One time there was a priest that had been in a bad accident and Dr Yaacoub had an inspiration to put in a filter in one of the priest's central lines and that prevented clots from traveling to his brain.

Thank you, Erwin. She is so frail and weakened. I hope that she starts eating more now.

Love,

MARY FADERAN

Agnes

March 8, 2011

Hi Annette,

Yes, I will let you know. It might be tomorrow or Thursday. dad said the dr was leaning towards tomorrow.

Do you know how to get to St E East? It's on Creasy Lane, after the main road McCarty Rd or St. If you are coming down 52 going south, turn left on Greenbush Ave, then right on Creasy Lane. Keep on Creasy until you pass McCarty. On the left is Unity medical center and then after that is St Elizabeth East. Park at the Visitor's entrance, go to the elevators on the right after the main doors, go to the 2nd floor, turn left to 2 South. She's in room 22.

MOM'S LAST DAYS

Love to you all,

Mary

March 8, 2011

Hi Ronette,

Maraming salamat *[thank you]*. I am glad you said that about Dr Y. I know he wants to help my Mom. Dr Gudapati talked to me kanina *[sometime ago]* and he was not so sold on the plans for angiogram. I told him that we know Dr Y's abilities and that he has done Dad's angiogram. So Dr G said ok let him do the angiogram.

Anyway I am hoping and trusting in God's providence that He will give Mom the graces she needs to be healed.

Thanks, Mary

March 8, 2011

MOM'S LAST DAYS

Oh, please come! Visitors are medicine too. Today Mom looked so much better especially since she got visitors from our Pinoy friends who are working also at St E. even her nurse commented on how much better she looked since the nurse came on duty this morning! So, we are happy about the fact that you will be coming!

Mary

March 8, 2011

Hello,

Today Mom seemed to be stronger and also had several visitors. Her hospitalist told me that she didn't really have a heart attack but only an ischemic event. He also said her troponin levels have decreased (the marker for cardiac tissue damage) and seems that her "event" happened within 24 hrs of when she had chest pain. So it was - to him - not a big event.

Mom is still a little shy about eating though. She feels the pressure to eat. I don't know how to make her want to eat.

They are going to have her go for a CT scan tonight and if needed they will do a thoracocentisis (sp) tomorrow where they will aspirate (with a fine needle) fluid from her chest cavity.

Such a lot of goings on! I do hope she will be strong and safeguarded through these procedures.

One more thing she will go through is the angiogram. Her cardiologist wants her to rest a couple of days before he puts her through it.

She is still on the TPN and that is so helpful. Dad tells me that we don't have to go look for an ECF since the surgeon said she can stay here till she is discharged. So that is good news too!

MOM'S LAST DAYS

I think that is all I know right now. I am hoping for a good night's sleep tonight. Good night and sleep well!

Mary

March 8, 2011

Hi Rheeda,

No, she won't go to an ECF. Her surgeon assured her she will recover and be discharged from St E. So that is a weight off our shoulders:-).

Love,

Mary

March 8, 2011

Mom passed a quiet night. She was on O2 and not on the bipap machine. This morning her nurse said her CO2 blood level was a little elevated. They took an arterial blood gas sample and that also bore out the lab result. So they put her back on the bipap machine. She said she still felt awful. Now the respiratory tech is here to give her some therapy.

I am waiting to see her dr to visit.

Let us pray she will feel much better soon!

Mary

March 8, 2011

Hi Dan,

You are most welcome to visit Mom. She

MOM'S LAST DAYS

will be glad to see you. You will be like good medicine and lift up her spirits:)

Mary

PS room 22 in 2South, second floor.

March 8, 2011

Hello again!

Mom will be having a ct scan this evening so I am not so sure whether she will be here when you visit. Maybe you can visit her next week?

Mary

MARY FADERAN

March 8, 2011

Dear Marilu,

My Dad and I fine. My Mom just had a light breakfast and she is a little better and more talkative today:-) Her vital

signs are good. Her cardiologist might do an angioplasty this afternoon. He has not decided for sure. Some of our friends that work in St E have dropped by and this has also animated my Mom. We are so fortunate to have such wonderful and prayerful friends! And most of them are because they love my Mom, who is such a people person!

I am waiting for my Dad to come back to relieve me so that I can go to work too.

Rosemary and Suzanne came by last evening and that was just wonderful.

Love,Mary

MOM'S LAST DAYS

MARY FADERAN

March 9, 2011

Hello,

Mom went through a thoracentesis procedure about an hour ago. I saw her dr afterwards and he said they aspirated 500 mls of fluid from each side of her chest cavity (pleural space). That's a whopping liter! He said that she should breathe better now.

She is in and out of sleep, her vital signs are good.

She's asking for some Pinoy food like mango juice and puto. So I will go to the Asia store to get her some. That's pretty good, don't you think?

BTW they don't allow real flowers in CCU so if you really want to send or bring flowers the fake kind is ok:-)

Best,

Mary

MOM'S LAST DAYS

March 9, 2011

Hi Jenny,

I think my Mom would be ok to see you. I don't know what the schedule for Friday is yet but if there's a change (eg

procedures or tests) I will let you know.

March 9, 2011

Hi,

The ultrasound tech is here looking at Mom's arm because it looks swollen and red. They want to make sure that it isn't a clot but just a 'third space' (med term that might mean edema maybe). I had been saying a stream of Hail Marys while the ultrasound is happening. Pray that this is not a clot.

She will be having her angiogram on Friday. Not sure what time, so please hold off your visits till Saturday.

Her thoracoscentesis was today and they collected a liter of fluid from her chest. Her lung dr said she should be

breathing much better.

Mom did have a little meal today: cracker dipped in coffee and some chocolate pudding. I got her the mango drink but she wanted to delay drinking this.

Until the next email,

Mary

March 10, 2011

Hello all,

Just a short email:

Dad called and said that the angiogram is scheduled for 12 noon tomorrow (Friday). The lung doc also came by and said that he

MOM'S LAST DAYS

is satisfied with Mom's state of her lungs. He said that if everything goes well with tomorrow's angiogram, he will be signing off Mom's case.

A friend at work said to me that Mom will be undergoing cardiac rehab, so that will also be at St E, most likely.

I also called Mom's nurse earlier today since I couldn't get a hold of Dad's cell. The nurse said Mom is doing good and that she was having her PICC line re-placed.

I am now going to get some stuff from home to bring so I can just go straight to work tomorrow and leave in good time to be with the parents for tomorrow's procedure.

Love to you all and God bless!

Mary

March 11, 2011

MARY FADERAN

Hello,

Mom's cardiologist dropped by. He said that all three of her coronary arteries have blockages but they fixed the culprit today. He said that he did not do the other two c. Arteries today bec it would have used a lot of dye and that would be too much for her kidneys, so he said he will do the others in a couple of weeks. So the question is will she stay over the next two weeks in the hospital or go back for the second procedure? We didn't get to ask him bec he got called to the ER. Dr Yaacoub said that the second procedure would be ok.

So that is how it is at this time. We are grateful and happy at any rate.

Love,

Mary

MOM'S LAST DAYS

March 11, 2011

The artery with the most blockage. She has had such a lot of stress but I think that the prayers of her loved ones are sustaining her. And of course she knows that we are with her through each step. Again we are very grateful for everyone's prayers.

March 11, 2011

Hi Susana,

I gave my Mom your message. She was very happy.

Thank you for your prayers. I am so glad that her dr could help her. I was very anxious about today because it seemed a lot for her to go through. But her cardiologist is so very good.

Praise God and all His Saints!

MARY FADERAN

Mary

March 11, 2011

Aura,

Thanks so much for your prayers:-)

God bless,

Mary

PS I have made a note of Ate Letty's address. I think she wrote me a while ago.

March 11, 2011

Dear Tita Baby,

I do remember you! So good to hear from you! yes, I told Mom this morning that you wrote and you are all praying for

MOM'S LAST DAYS

her. God willing she will be on her feet and glad to be home with us soon!

How are Jay and Jennifer? They're probably grown and have their own families, ano *[right]*?

Love,

Agnes

March 11, 2011

Tonight Mom had pain in her leg and foot (the one where they did the catheter) and it took a longish time to have the nurse come to give her pain meds. I wasn't very happy about this as her nurse was with another patient. I thought that my Mom had already asked for the med and the nurse did not return, but when her nurse came back she said she was with another patient. I don't think I was too popular tonight with the nurses here. I asked one if they thought they would be understaffed this weekend and he said he didn't think so. Anyway they finally gave Mom her meds including the pain meds. I would just wish there was some sort of continuity in her care. Of course she isn't the only patient in CCU but having gotten through a cardiac cath today should have made a little difference. Anyway, I hope this weekend will be better than last weekend was in terms of the quality of the nursing staff. Her nurses have been good but I'm not so excited about the ones on tonight.

March 11, 2011

Hello,

Mom's nurse came to tell us that they are done with the procedure. By God's grace they placed 3 stents in Mom's heart. She has not yet come back to her room but will shortly. I am so amazed at modern medicine and esp cardiology. The nurse

MOM'S LAST DAYS

(oh she just came in!) said she did good. Mom is fine and she said she is very tire. So I think she will be snoozing for the rest of the day. Her nurse is pretty darn efficient! I truly like their efficiency and care for Mom.

I am so grateful to the Lord and His Mother for their most loving care for Mom and for my Dad and me.

Thank you too for your care and prayers. Please send this to the others whose emails I don't have.

Love,

Mary

March 11, 2011

Hello Ate Letty,

Thank you so much for your prayers. I mentioned your good wishes to Mom and she said she really appreciates your prayers for her.

I'll keep you posted.

March 11, 2011

Hi,

More on Mom's cardiac procedure.

Love,

Agnes/Tita

March 11, 2011

Hi Judy,

Maraming salamat! Yes, God is The Doctor and I am sure He is taking good care of my Mom.

MOM'S LAST DAYS

Thank you again!

Mary

March 12, 2011

Dear Cousins,

I just wanted to tell you how glad we are that you visited Mom and us today. I also want to thank you for your generosity. You are just the best! And Mom has definitely benefited from your presence. She is pretty alert even tho she has her eyes closed.

I will surely continue to keep you abreast of what is up and so on.

Love you all,

Mary

PS Please give Timm a hug from us three. Hope he is doing well!

MARY FADERAN

March 13, 2011

Hello,

Mom woke me up at 12:30 am this morning wanting to get out of bed, so her nurses were happy to put her in the chair. Luckily Dad was at home or he would be out of a sleeping place. Mom's bp was good, too. They are hoping that with her sitting on the chair she will progress in her rehabilitation. One thing more is that Dr Y will want to do her other coronary arteries in 6-8 wks time. So that will be when she's already been released to home. She also had a little applesauce and mashed potatoes last evening for dinner.

A number of VIPs came to visit her yesterday including our dear friends from Indy and our dear cousins from S. Bend and Chicago, then a surprise visit from Dr Chua and her Mom and sister-in-law Fe bearing gifts of food from the Rosary group meeting. Also A--- and his wife from Blessed Sacrament dropped by, saying how much they missed seeing us at 10:30 am Mass.

Her nurses in the last 24 hrs have been super and caring, and they also have cautioned the other techs who come to take her xray or whatever that she must be treated with care due to her skin being so fragile.

She is still on TPN, although they say they want to wean her off it.

She is off the O2 now and doing well.

I think that is all for now.

Have a blessed Sunday!

Mary

March 13, 2011

Mom had a little too much of a med and

had gotten confused today, and that med also causes nausea and vomiting.

She also had a fever which went up to 101.5 at which point they gave her tylenol and it went down to 101.1. She is resting sleeping and now she had pain in her ankle so they are going to give her a pain med (pill). She indicated that she will try to swallow a pill, so that is good. I think she might have had a reaction either to the blood transx, the active week before or any number of things and she may be just also tired out still. Anyway, we are all praying she gets over whatever is causing her fever.

I also wanted to thank our Rosary group friends for their wonderful care packages.

Till the next update,

God bless!

Mary

PS She was able to take her pain meds just now. Her nurse is glad. So am I.

MOM'S LAST DAYS

MARY FADERAN

March 13, 2011

Dad is holding steady.

Yes, most of the time nurses are ok and they communicate well with us.

Mom has a slight fever today so they are keeping tabs on that. She's been sleeping all morning.

I went home yesterday to just hang, take walk/run around the neighborhood, and iron some clothes before heading back to the hospital. The thing is they don't have their main cafeteria open on wkends so we either order room service, go get fast food or rely on the care packages we get from friends.

Thanks for the advice. We are blessed to have you and everyone else who is praying.

MOM'S LAST DAYS

Agnes

March 13, 2011

Thank you, Rheeda. I am very glad you all came to visit. Yes, Mom had quite a lot to go through. She really needs to get more rest. I think at her age a nice bit of rest will be needed after last Friday's procedure. I hope and pray she will have caring drs and nurses who will be patient enough.

BTW her fever is down to 100. I am happy about that! Her BP is 116/64. That's good too!

If you ever want to call me my cell is ---.

Love,
Mary

March 14, 2011

Hi All,

Dad and I each had a talk with Dr May. Dad saw her at the hospital while she called me on the phone. She was very good and said that they will be reviewing her chart, talk to Dr Y, and also talk with Mom and to determine what the short term and long term goals are. She said that patients that are Mom's age tend to have longer recuperative times, which I agreed with. She said that she will be addressing the symptoms that Mom is exhibiting (esp the delirium that Mom is experiencing at this time). She asked me about Mom's normal activities in a day, her interests etc. Dr May gave me her cell no. and said that I can reach her 24/7 to ask any question that I might have. I am glad that Dr May is caring for Mom as Dr May has a huge reputation in the hospital as being an patient advocate, and also she terrifies the nursing staff because she gets people to really sit up and do their job and not slack off. So that is a big thing to me, someone who will work to make Mom better. I had been apprehensive about talking to Dr May but after she and I had a chat, I felt so much more relieved.

Thanks again for the support, everyone. Dad also sounded good when he talked to me after he saw Dr May, so that is a good sign that everyone wants Mom to get well.

Love,

Mary

March 14, 2011

Hello,

Mom's temperature is still going, 100.8 at the last time I asked (this a.m.). Dr Yaacoub just called me and expressed his concerns about Mom. He said her resistance is low, and he thinks that he will need the help of another Dr, Dr May (a very good one) to oversee and review Mom's care. He said that he is not recommending that they hold or discontinue treatment but that Dr May will

be able to help in Mom's care. He said that
he is feeling discouraged that when they
fix one thing another thing breaks down.
They are treating her with multiple
antibiotics at this time. I will let you know
what Dr May says once she has seen Mom.
Please keep your prayers going at this
time. I think that Mom's [sic] is
recuperating slowly and maybe it is still
too early to tell how her condition is going.
I believe that the doctors and nurses are
running low on patience.

Thank you again for your thoughts and prayers,

Mary

March 14, 2011

I know, she's elderly, she recovers slow
and with everything she's already had, it's a
real miracle that she is still here. Dr May is
(I believe) the sort of doctor you mention.

MOM'S LAST DAYS

She's got a huge rep in the hospital and has also seen Mom one time when Mom was in the hospital for her heart arrhythmia. So, I am hoping that Dr May won't sound the alarm and give up yet. I am also thinking that there are meds that they have given Mom that cause her to probably not 'catch up'. I don't think Dr Y's expertise extends further than the heart, so he is wise to ask Dr May for help.

I will let you know how things develop. I was feeling this dread today that I will be getting a phone call from the hospital, just because of how her nurse was yesterday and also because these people tend to want to seeresults [sic] fast, and since Mom is not as young as their average patient might be, they don't know how best to gauge. I don't know if I'm making sense.

Thanks for your thoughts, Glenda. I will keep them in mind when Dr May talks to me.

Mary

MARY FADERAN

March 14, 2011

She is still feeling the effects of her procedure and also perhaps her meds are getting in the way of her being able to get out of this state. Dr May explained that it happens when someone like Mom who has had several things happen to her might be run down. See my other email about Dr May.

As for the stress, I'm coping enough (maybe). I do tend to keep it in but I do have a therapist that I still see every 3 weeeks [sic] and he is aware of what Mom is going through. I try to get out and exercise (not a lot). I don't know how long I can sleep in Mom's room every day (even Dad) without getting run down. At least lately Mom has been sleeping most of the night, so that gives us some time to really sleep.

Love,

Ag

MOM'S LAST DAYS

March 14, 2011

I had been told that Mom spent the day sleeping and that at times was difficult to rouse but when I arrived from work to be here at the hospital she was awake, and looked like she was following the goings on. She asked me how long she had been in CCU. I guess it was a lot of stuff that went on that she could not or would not process. I explained to her how she got here and she looked pretty surprised. Her temp is back to normal (thank God) and the delirium is gone although she says that "they wrapped her body in plastic" possibly due to the shiny look on her arms and fingers that have become swollen - something that she has developed and her drs are treating her for that.

She [sic] had some choc pudding tonight, and we shared an orange - although she didn't care for the pulp. She doesn't like the food she is getting and I don't blame her. I said she needs to think of something she would like so that I can get it for her.

MARY FADERAN

She is back on O2 as a precaution.

Dr May, the dr I spoke with on the phone, is taking on Mom's case. She was asked by Dr Y as a consult. She is going to be seeing Mom (or one of her group) every day to follow her case. She told me that she will determine Mom's short term and long term goals and treat her symptoms and help to improve Mom's recovery. She says that it will take longer for Mom to recover which I agree with. Anyway, we talked a little about Mom's iv nutrition as I had wondered about her blood sugar. But she put my concerns to rest.

Well, it is a nice end to the day. Mom is not delirious now, fever gone and she's had a little bit to eat.

On that note, I wish you all good night.

Mary

March 14, 2011

MOM'S LAST DAYS

Dear Sr Ann,

Yes, thank God she has a more positive state today. I left her this morning a little snoozy but she was already awake by 5 am since she wanted to use the bedpan. I agree, Dr May is a great name as well as person. She is Catholic, and signed the Pro-Life advertisement before on the newspaper. Dr May is Director of Palliative Care in St Elizabeth. I am glad she is on Mom's case, since I recognize her from my past employment there, and her reputation is very good. She is truly an advocate for patients and is experienced in Internal Medicine.

As for flowers, you may send flowers but not the real ones as it is not allowed in CCU. She will be so happy to receive anything from you, Sr. Ann!

I think that she needs to be encouraged in her recovery, as she still feels a little cowed by all that has happened to her. She had a scary time when she suffered respiratory distress last Monday, and then they stuck needles on both of her sides to remove fluid, and then they put three stents in her coronary artery.

That really takes a lot out of a person ordinarily, and for Mom, at her age and the fact that she has not had a lot of food to eat (although she is on iv nutrition, which helps) those have made it hard to feel like the coast is clear on the road to recovery. I think, though, that having talked to Dr May, who has given us a ray of hope that someone is watching out for Mom, I feel a little more relieved for the time that Mom is at St E. Dr May wants Mom to improve and get to the point where she was before she got hospitalized, or even before that when she was actually doing what she loved to do, writing for our MTA, cooking recipes that she got from TV shows or cookbooks, and going out with us to the bookstore to just sit, drink some coffee/tea, and check out more books about our Faith and cooking.

Thank you so much, Sr Ann, for your cheerful email.

MOM'S LAST DAYS

Love,

Mary

March 14, 2011

Hi All,

Dad and I each had a talk with Dr
May. Dad saw her at the hospital
while she called me on the phone. She was
very good and said that they will be
reviewing her chart, talk to Dr Y, and also
talk with Mom and to determine what the
short term and long term goals are. She
said that patients that are Mom's age tend
to have longer recuperative times, which I
agreed with. She said that she will be
addressing the symptoms that Mom is
exhibiting (esp the delirium that Mom is
experiencing at this time). She asked
me about Mom's normal activities in a day,
her interests etc. Dr May gave me her cell
no. and said that I can reach her 24/7 to ask

any question that I might have. I am glad that Dr May is caring for Mom as Dr May has a huge reputation in the hospital as being an patient advocate, and also she terrifies the nursing staff because she gets people to really sit up and do their job and not slack off. So that is a big thing to me, someone who will work to make Mom better. I had been apprehensive about talking to Dr May but after she and I had a chat, I felt so much more relieved.

Thanks again for the support, everyone. Dad also sounded good when he talked to me after he saw Dr May, so that is a good sign that everyone wants Mom to get well.

Love,

Mary

March 15, 2011

MOM'S LAST DAYS

Dear Sr Ann,

Yes, thank God she has a more positive state today. I left her this morning a little snoozy but she was already awake by 5 am since she wanted to use the bedpan. I agree, Dr May is a great name as well as person. She is Catholic, and signed the Pro-Life advertisement before on the newspaper. Dr May is Director of Palliative Care in St Elizabeth. I am glad she is on Mom's case, since I recognize her from my past employment there, and her reputation is very good. She is truly an advocate for patients and is experienced in Internal Medicine.

As for flowers, you may send flowers but not the real ones as it is not allowed in CCU. She will be so happy to receive anything from you, Sr. Ann!

I think that she needs to be encouraged in her recovery, as she still feels a little cowed by all that has happened to her. She had a scary time when she suffered respiratory distress last Monday, and then they stuck needles on both of her sides to remove fluid, and then they put three stents in her coronary artery.

That really takes a lot out of a person ordinarily, and for Mom, at her age and the fact that she has not had a lot of food to eat (although she is on iv nutrition, which helps) those have made it hard to feel like the coast is clear on the road to recovery. I think, though, that having talked to Dr May, who has given us a ray of hope that someone is watching out for Mom, I feel a little more relieved for the time that Mom is at St E. Dr May wants Mom to improve and get to the point where she was before she got hospitalized, or even before that when she was actually doing what she loved to do, writing for our MTA, cooking recipes that she got from TV shows or cookbooks, and going out with us to the bookstore to just sit, drink some coffee/tea, and check out more books about our Faith and cooking.

Thank you so much, Sr Ann, for your cheerful email.

MOM'S LAST DAYS

Love,

Mary

March 15, 2011

Mom is sleeping this evening having had a few things done today including sitting on the chair. She looks better, and has already become descriptive about how they got her to sit on the chair - "herculean" - she said. She is off the O2, and I think that her vitals are ok. She has not eaten today, but the TPN is ongoing. They would like to have her move her bowels but so far just wind. She did complain of a stomachache and it could be that she may be doing a No. 2 at some point. I overheard her nurse say that they plan to do an abdominal ultrasound tomorrow.

Dr May has ordered that Mom sit on the

chair 3x today, but Mom did it once although she was on it for 2 hours. I think that this is a good start.

Other than these tidbits, I don't know anything more. If Mom wakes up sometime this evening I can ask her about how her day went.

A nice Mass Card came for her from my SFO friend, Betty Price. Thank you, Betty! My SFO friends are all praying for Mom.

Well, that is it for now.

Mary

March 15, 2011

Mom is sleeping this evening having had a few things done today including sitting on the chair. She looks better, and has already become descriptive about how they got her to sit on the chair - "herculean" - she said. She is off the O2, and I think that her vitals are ok. She has not eaten today, but the TPN is ongoing. They would like to have her move her bowels but so far just wind. She did complain of a stomachache and it could be that she may be doing a No. 2 at some point. I overheard her nurse say that they plan to do an abdominal ultrasound tomorrow.

Dr May has ordered that Mom sit on the chair 3x today, but Mom did it once although she was on it for 2 hours. I think that this is a good start.

Other than these tidbits, I don't know anything more. If Mom wakes up sometime this evening I can ask her about how her day went.

A nice Mass Card came for her from my SFO friend, Betty Price. Thank you, Betty! My SFO friends are all praying for Mom.

Well, that is it for now.

Mary

MARY FADERAN

March 16, 2011

Hello,

We had a chat with Dr May. Mom had a not so hot day today, drowsy and not wanting to do pt, and having nausea

and vomiting. She also vomited while Dr May was with us. So Dr May said that they will only give iv meds for now give Mom's tummy a break, and slowly introduce liquids until she can handle soft foods. Dr May thought this would be for the remainder of the week. I asked her about rehab, and she said perhaps by next week.

So I got a call from Sharon from Mulberry and she said that Mom was accepted there. I asked Sharon how far they were and she said they were only 10 minutes from the mall. The Mall is about 20 min from our house. Sharon also visited Mom and Dad at the hospital. Dad also mentioned that someone from Cumberland Pointe came to see Mom, and said that they did not have any beds available at this time but they might when Mom is discharged. But I know that CP had already a rule not to accept TPN pts. However, if Mom's TPN is dc'd at her discharge then CP would be the better place bec it is accessible to my office (almost on the same street) and also to our house. CP used to be called George Davis Manor. Anyway, Dr May envisioned Mom being on soft foods perhaps by next week, and that she will not be on TPN at some point.

I am feeling optimistic that perhaps our hotel experience at St E will be soon ending and we will soon be close to home and each other.

Mom's temp is 100.3 at this time. She's resting, and I hope will have a quiet night.

I am glad Dr May got to talk to us tonight. She's very well regarded in the medical community.

MARY FADERAN

God bless and good night,

Mary

March 16, 2011

Hi Marilu,

I will pray for the vigil tomorrow. Thank you for your prayers for my Mom and Dad and me. I am still a little anxious whenever I am supposed to talk to Drs, but I guess it is the white coat syndrome.

I am hoping that with God's care and the hard work of the staff at St E everything will come out ok.

Love,

March 17, 2011

Hello,

MOM'S LAST DAYS

Well today it seems Mom had two PT sessions, one to have her sit on the edge of the bed and the other she sat on the other side. I noticed her hands weren't swollen as before, and she seemed to look better. She said that she walked all day and followed Dad to the train. I think she might be a bit medicated, IYKWIM.

Her nurse Bob, a more mature person, told her that they are going to make her strong enough to go to the rehab place. He added that his Mom just got out of the hospital and into a rehab and the first day they put her through a workout. Then Bob said that Mom will be ok.

Mom is on iv meds mostly. She still can't have even jello as it makes her want to vomit.

I am hoping Mom will sleep a good night's sleep tonight. Last night she roused Dad and me several times for various reasons.

I got another call from Sharon of Mulberry today. She was just touching base. She said she will call again next week.

I am hoping that Mom will be closer to being discharged then. I cannot believe March is almost over.

Have a blessed night:)

Mary

March 18, 2011

Hello Everyone,

Just an update to let you know that Mom is being transferred to Seton at St E Central campus. They will do

the move today at 4:30 pm. I am hoping that once she is there, she will continue in her recovery. Dad said that she had a PT session today and was able to sit on the edge of the bed, and also stand for a few seconds.

Dr May will continue to follow Mom at Seton, which I am very glad about. I think

MOM'S LAST DAYS

that this move is the better way to help Mom recover, rather than to go to Mulberry (which is farther) and/or to Cumberland since she is still on TPN.

I will keep you updated with any further developments.

God bless us all,

Mary

March 18, 2011

Hello,

Mom had a smooth transfer to Seton today. Her room no is 2315. Take the elevators at the 14th St entrance and turn left then right through the double doors. Her room is the first on the left.

She has the afternoon sun, and her room is bright and clean. I saw my old friend Dan who is now the pharmacist at Seton. He welcomed Mom and told us that they'll get her back on her feet. I am glad that someone I know and used to work with is here to watch her meds. Also Backy our dear friend and PT is working here and I'm sure he will keep an eye on Mom.

I am glad that everything worked out so she could be at Seton. We were told before that she didn't make the criteria for her to go there, or that there was no room.

We met her nurse and tech too and they are very nice.

Guess that is all for now, folks.

Till the next update, stay well and God bless!

Mary

March 18, 2011

Hi Glenda,

MOM'S LAST DAYS

I hope so too about Seton.

So far, our financial obligations have been manageable. I believe that Medicare is taking the most part of the expenses, and also Mom has AARP supplemental insurance. However, I need to talk to the social worker (unless Dad already has) about the ECF. I know from talking to the Cumberland Pointe and other ECFs, Medicare pays for 100% of the first 20 days in ECF, then they pay 80% afterwards. Dr May did say that for each day in the hospital, there are 3-4 days of rehab. So with Mom having been in the hospital for 2 weeks, x4 days = 56 days, so a couple of months.

Someone at work said that we might qualify for financial assistance from some place. I may have to go into Google etc to get info. Or, again, talk to the social worker. Kaya lang the social worker is kind of busy, so I hope that we can have a chance to discuss.

Thanks pala [by the way] for the pastries

you brought last time you visited. I particularly liked the scone. I'm a scone fan, anyway!

Mary

March 19, 2011

Hello,

Mom is taking a nap now, having had some sips of broth. She was

mumbling about something earlier but after Dr G came to see her she settled to a snorefest. Heasked her how she liked her new place and she said it was better.
So that isgood [sic] to hear. The Dr said that Mom can personalize her room. I don't know if they will allow us to put up pictures on the wall but we will think of something. The nurses say to keep personal belongings to a
minimum, though.

MOM'S LAST DAYS

Her rn also said the Mom had a bit of jello for breakfast when she checked her earlier. Her rn said she saw telltale bits of red around her lips.

This is short but I'll check in again later.

Mary

March 19, 2011

Hello Ann,

Just an update about Mom. She seems to like her new place. I think it is good that she arrived yesterday so she can

adjust to her new place before they have things to do for or with her.

I was so glad to sleep in my bed last night. I couldn't wake up today but did because I had a hair appointment. I felt so grateful to be somewhere nice and relaxing, and just to be back in my little town. I also went to a new coffee shop by us called Cafe Lumos. They serve sandwiches and scones and coffee. I had the basil pesto chicken sandwich and tomato bisque soup. Just wonderful and different from the food that I usually have.

Right now I am with Mom while she sleeps. She seemed a little uncomfortable earlier but then she settled down when her nurses changed her position.

Dad is having a little break for lunch and that is ok, for he needs some fresh air after almost 3 wks inside CCU.

I don't know whether we will go to Mass together or separately again. We might go to St E tomorrow at 9 am then go to see Mom right after.

It is just so pretty outside. When I went to my hair appt I passed by the Borders store. They are closing and it looks quite empty inside. I didn't bother to go inside.

MOM'S LAST DAYS

Well, I guess that is all.

I am attaching a picture I took after my hair appt.

Love,

Mary

March 19, 2011

Hi Holly,

Yes, we'll get those strips. It might be a good idea to have some pictures that will encourage her to cooperate in her therapy. Any suggestions are welcome!

Mary

MARY FADERAN

March 19, 2011

Hi Rheeda,
We are just finished saying the rosary and Mom has been snoozing most of the day. She just got her vitals taken and she is good. She doesn't have a fever and her bp is good.

Her room just has no extra bed for overnighters. Dad and I go home to sleep now. The nurses and aides take good care of her. I call in the am to see how Mom spent the night. We have told her nurses that we used to sleep with Mom at St E east and they assure us that she is in good hands.

Your Chinese resto sounds good! Is that in S Bend? We like to go out to two or three places. Our favorite is close to our home.

Tomorrow we will be here for the 9 am

MOM'S LAST DAYS

Mass at the chapel, then we will go to see Mom. Unfortunately there is no cafeteria open so we will likely go get our lunch somewhere.

I hope the weather is good tomorrow also. I hope our roses will come up this season. I forgot to cover our newest rose last winter, so it might not be too happy now.

Well, that is it for now. Have a lovely evening!

Mary

March 19, 2011

Hi Rheeda,
We are just finished saying the rosary and Mom has been snoozing most of the day. She just got her vitals taken and she is good. She doesn't have a fever and her bp is good.

MARY FADERAN

Her room just has no extra bed for overnighters. Dad and I go home to sleep now. The nurses and aides take good care of her. I call in the am to see how Mom spent the night. We have told her nurses that we used to sleep with Mom at St E east and they assure us that she is in good hands.

Your Chinese resto sounds good! Is that in S Bend? We like to go out to two or three places. Our favorite is close to our home.

Tomorrow we will be here for the 9 am Mass at the chapel, then we will go to see Mom. Unfortunately there is no cafeteria open so we will likely go get our lunch somewhere.

I hope the weather is good tomorrow also. I hope our roses will come up this season. I forgot to cover our newest rose last winter, so it might not be too happy now.

Well, that is it for now. Have a lovely

MOM'S LAST DAYS

evening!

Mary

March 19, 2011

Thank you, Ronette, for your great advice, friendship and most especially your prayers.

Mary

March 19, 2011

We opted for some Chinese tonight. I am beat tonight. Currently doing laundry and catching up on news.

Oh, btw we prayed the rosary before going home. Then Dad gave Mom a blessing. They do that every night, bless each other and then me (usually already in my bed by that time).

Have a good night:)
Mary

March 19, 2010

Dan and Po-Ching,

Thank you! Yes, you certainly may visit. Rm 2315 enter by the 14th St entrance. Go up to the 2nd floor up the first

elevator turn left then right go thru double doors her room is first on left.

Mary

March 19, 2011

Dear Susana,

The visiting hours are really relaxed and

MOM'S LAST DAYS

you can go anytime. I think she will be glad to see you. She is a little sleepy

during this weekend because of her meds, though, but maybe on Monday they will start with PT and she may be

more alert then.

Love,

Mary

March 20, 2011

We went to 9 am Mass at St E Central Chapel then went to see Mom. She was so glad to see us, and was under the

impression that we travelled far to visit her. She asked us how long we were going to visit and then later said we should go or else "they" will ask us to go. I assured her that she is much closer to our home than the first hospital, that we will stay as long as we want, and that no one will make us leave. I think she may have slept through some of the events and conversations of the past couple of days (her move to Seton). She is perkier today, and that is good to see. She did have an unsuccesful [sic] meal at breakfast (threw up) so she is npo for the day. Her Dr G visited and he

ordered xrays of her chest and belly to rule out any problems with respect to aspiration of stomach contents and ileus. Now she is taking a nap and Dad is catching up on sleep.

Mom has already had two visitors today and we are told that more will be coming later.

We were concerned that she might be missing us at night but she said she slept well last night. I called her nurse earlier this am and she said that Mom took half her pill last night. I think she tends to choose what she can take and we have

MOM'S LAST DAYS

encouraged her to be as compliant as she can to make her recovery that much sooner from hospital.

I am also encouraged that her sleeping is more normal. Before she would be mumbling in her sleep, and would wake up in fits and starts, wanting relief or asking for prayers. Today she's napping like she would at home, drawing the covers over her and curling up.

We are always grateful for each day that Mom is feeling better. I am hoping that the meds she takes for the stents will not make her nausea and vomiting worse (the side effects) and maybe they can dial down the dose to some degree that will be suitable for her weight.

Mary

March 21, 2011

Hello Eileen,

MARY FADERAN

Your prayers along with others are being heard, for sure. I know that after all this, that Mom is now convalescing at Seton, God is truly present (and hears us) and I am so glad that there are friends also at Seton that are looking out for Mom. God's mercy is always providential. It is inspiring to us how God truly works in mysterious ways.

I have been worried about how Seton will be for Mom. Yesterday she said she wanted to go back to the hospital, a little confused about where she was. Dr May said that confusion can occur in elderly patients, and they are aware of that. I just talked to Dad and they are now treating Mom for physical therapy - and our dear friend Fred is her therapist (he's Pinoy). They are sitting her on the chair for 30 minutes after letting her sit on the edge of her bed. I am praying that she will tolerate all this.

Let's keep on praying - and trusting in God's love.

MOM'S LAST DAYS

Love,

Agnes

March 21, 2011

I am sitting by Mom's bed while she snoozes. Her NP was here and talked a little bit with us. Mom had a good session with her PT today and has reached Level 2 of her goal mountain. She sat on the edge of her bed and on a chair. She will do this daily and the thought is that it will help resolve her ileus problem. They also think that once that is resolved she can start eating real food again. Right now she is npo except for some oral meds. Today is a good day overall. She's getting better.

She does have some confusion though and it is probably because of her being in hospital so long, and the time and places tend to blur. The NP says that they are watching this and thinks that once she gets into PT she will become more attuned to her surroundings.

Mom still needs to get some sleep time in, since she has been up the last couple nights.

I am feeling good about today and hopeful for her recovery. A coworker said his Dad went to Seton after he had a stroke and he regained the ability to walk at Seton. So that speaks to Seton's staff!

Well, I better end here and hope to give you more news tomorrow!

Mary

March 21, 2011

Dear Julia,

I received your letter today and the wonderful wallet keepsakes from St Padre Pio. Mom has been asking me about this

MOM'S LAST DAYS

item (a friend of mine had something for her that was similar) and I assured Mom that it was in her purse. She doesn't have a secure place to put it in her room, and also we found it precarious to pin medals to her hospital gown as it has a way of getting tossed in the laundry and then getting lost. The last time it happened, one of the nurses was able to retrieve her holy medals only because it happened over the weekend and the laundry service did not come to collect dirty laundry that time. But, I will certainly show Mom today when I go to her hospital.

She is now on her fourth day at Seton Hospital. I called my Dad earlier (he's with her) and he said that the physical therapists were there at the time and they had been working with Mom. Also the nurse had come to give her some pills, so that may mean that Mom is now perhaps able to take pills by mouth. My Dad had to end the phone call since he was in the middle of all this. I hesitate to call again, mostly because I am afraid that she might have vomited again or something and I just get so

MARY FADERAN

worried.

I really need to stop worrying, like St Padre Pio always said to never worry. God has taken care of us all (especially Mom) throughout this very scary and stressful experience and now that Mom is in a very good, caring place, God will surely be present in everything there.

Thank you again, Julia, for your prayers and for the prayers of everyone there for Mom. I am sure that in time Mom will be rehabilitated and be able to come home soon.

Mary

MOM'S LAST DAYS

March 22, 2011

Well Mom had been given ativan last night for restlessness and today she wasn't exactly good and not exactly bad.

She was harder to understand. They did CT scans on her head and abdomen. Both came back ok. There was less gas in her belly. She seems to be burping a bit which is good. She does have a yeast infection UTI. They are giving her antibiotics for that. Her temp is good, bp and hr good. She weighs 6 lbs more than when she came to Seton. I don't know how reliable that is but if that is true that's great. We were worried about her a bit tonighjt [sic] as she had pain in her feet and back. We took her 'boots' off (they are supposed to ease her pressure ulcer in her heels) and just put a pillow under her legs. She seemed to relax after that and once the pain meds took hold. We asked the nurses not to give her any more ativan. Oh and OT and PT came today but they didn't give her a lot to do, just leg and arm exercises. I do also note that Mom seemed more awake when I came in. She seemed interested in my stories about work.

We hope that she is a little better tomorrow and that the effect of the ativan will be worn off.

It's been a long day for Mom. We prayed the rosary and Dad gave her her nightly blessing before we went home.

Mary

March 23, 2011

Dear Ro,

You are most welcome to visit! I told Mom you wrote. She is still a bit sleepy today. Hopefully she will be more alert soon!

Mary

MOM'S LAST DAYS

March 23, 2011

Hello,

They decided to aspirate Mom's stomach contents this evening. The surgeon said she should feel better once it is done. He also said that they thought she has a liver abscess but he doesn't have the scan images to verify. In case there is they will try to do a liver aspiration but that is still something to determine. The Dr on her case just came in and said that this 'abscess' could also be a gall bladder 'spill' due to her operation. The surgeon who operated on her will be here tomorrow.

March 23, 2011

MARY FADERAN

Hello,

I just spoke with Dad and he said that Mom is sleeping most of the morning. Her nurse mentioned that her stomach seems more bloated than before. Anyway, in an earlier call this morning the nurse said that Mom vomited last night but spent a good night sleeping. She has a temp of 100.1, but altogether her vitals are good.

I'm not sure whether they are giving her any more po meds as a result of this vomiting.

I'll try to update you again later on when I've seen her after I get off work.

Blessings,

Mary

March 23, 2011

Holly,

MOM'S LAST DAYS

Please pray that she doesn't have a liver abscess.

Thanks,

Mary

March 23, 2011

Hello,

My Mom had a drop in bp today. They took blood cultures and another CT scan. They were able to get her bp back up. She's awake now but in some pain. They just gave her pain meds now. Her NP was here and looked at her and said she will have Dr May come and see her.

Mom has been getting pain in her feet mostly due to the pressure ulcer and also bec those boots are put on tight so we loosened them.

They changed her antibiotics too. We are

hopeful that things will get better.

Thank you for the continued prayers.

Mary

March 24, 2011

Hi,

I just wanted to let you know that Dr May has given Dad and me a not too happy prognosis for Mom. Dr

May said that the blockage in my Mom's intestine is quite definite, and that she needs surgery but that surgery would be too much for Mom at her weak condition. She said that we need to determine whether we want them to do all they can do for Mom (including ventilator) or to make Mom "comfortable". So, I am really feeling very sad and so is Dad at this situation. A friend of mine suggested that I ask for a second opinion, and someone at

MOM'S LAST DAYS

work (she my HR person) called Dr Cline (he's a GI guy at Arnett) to see if he can look at Mom's situation and if he can't do it himself, suggest someone else. I don't want to give up on Mom. I know that she is still aware and really is still involved with what is happening with her. I don't want to throw in the towel at all.

I'm hoping that God will make a miracle and have Mom back home soon. I hope things will look better too, but without a surgical intervention I am not sure how things will go.

Right now, MOm is still attached to a nasogastric tube where they still drain some of her stomach fluids, and also able to put through her po meds. I don't know whether this tube is still needed since she is having a problem with breathing with it. Dr May focused on the breathing problem and said this was the beginning of Mom's problem - she called it respiratory failure. It sounds grim, doesn't it? so you can imagine how Dad and I are feeling now.

MARY FADERAN

Mary

March 24, 2011

Hello,

We just talked to Mom's surgeon. He reviewed her chart and scans and said that he wants to drain her liver abscess, reposition her ng tube bec he thinks it could be kinked, and see whether they can put a dye in her stomach to see whether she really has this blockage. The issue also is that she seems to be losing blood somewhere and it is why they have tranfused her today. Her BP has been a little iffy but later on has improved. I was very heartened by Dr Jefson's plan to get Mom to feel better. I am hoping what he does will restart Mom's recovery. He is a well recommended surgeon too. A problem solver. He did say that if they do see a blockage it is too much to do surgery and we will have to make her comfortable.

It has been a long day. I think though that

MOM'S LAST DAYS

Dr J gives us hope.

Love,

Mary

March 24, 2011

Hi Ronette,

I hope that you can see your email.

Dad and I just chatted with Dr May. She thinks that the chances of Mom getting better are the same as her getting worse. If you have a chance, could you call me? My number is ---.

Thanks,

Mary

MARY FADERAN

MOM'S LAST DAYS

March 24, 2011

Hello,

We just talked to Mom's surgeon. He reviewed her chart and scans and said that he wants to drain her liver abscess, reposition her ng tube bec he thinks it could be kinked, and see whether they can put a dye in her stomach to see whether she really has this blockage. The issue also is that she seems to be losing blood somewhere and it is why they have tranfused her today. Her BP has been a little iffy but later on has improved. I was very heartened by Dr Jefson's plan to get Mom to feel better. I am hoping what he does will restart Mom's recovery. He is a well recommended surgeon too. A problem solver. He did say that if they do see a blockage it is too much to do surgery and we will have to make her comfortable.

It has been a long day. I think though that

Dr J gives us hope.

Love,

Mary

March 24, 2011

Just FYI they moved Mom to the first floor to room 1344. Her nurse suggested the move so that she would have more eyes to check her. Dr Jefson championed the move.

Mary

March 24, 2011

MOM'S LAST DAYS

Hi Rheeda,
She's still at Seton. Her room does not have an extra place to sleep.

We are pretty drained by today's events. God willing tomorrow will be better.

Good night,
Mary

March 24, 2011

Dear Nan,

Yes He is. Like a dear nun told me - God has the last word!

Amen,

Mary

March 25, 2011

MARY FADERAN

Hello Dear Ones,

Mom passed away this morning. She died on the Feast of the Assumption. Dad and I were at her side at the end.

She is now in Heaven. We are desolated that she is gone but we rejoice knowing that she is still with all of us in spirit.

Let us give thanks to God and His Mother for calling Mom home today.

God bless us all,

Mary

PS. Funeral at Soller Baker WL.

Not sure yet when Mass will be.

March 25, 2011

Sorry it is the Feast of the Annunciation.

MOM'S LAST DAYS

March 25, 2011

Hello,

The visitation and rosary will be on Monday from 5 to 8 and Mass at 10:00 on Tuesday. Dad and I went to the funeral home today and the notice will be in tomorrow's paper. I wish we wrote of Mom's love for Jesus and Mother Mary in the obit but Dad and I were just not in our right thoughts. We are just feeling rudderless right now. Mom was our organizer, leader and focus and now that she's not with us it seems very surreal. Our trip to Walmart today seemed weird, and Dad commented that we won't be getting Mom's meds or Boost anymore. It was sad.

Well, I know many of you won't be able to come and we understand. We know that you would come if possible. Dad and I are just glad to know your thoughts and prayers are for us. We have been carried by them throughout Mom's struggles in the last few months. Thank you once again for your love and prayers and your words of comfort.

It's been a long day. I hope everyone has a restful weekend.

Love,

Mary

March 25, 2011

Hello Dear Ones,
Mom passed away this morning. She died on the Feast of the Assumption. Dad and I were at her side at the end. She is now in Heaven. We are desolated that she is gone

MOM'S LAST DAYS

but we rejoice knowing that she is still with all of us in spirit. Let us give thanks to God and His Mother for calling Mom home today.

God bless us all,
Mary

PS. Funeral at Soller Baker WL. Not sure yet when Mass will be.

March 25, 2011

Dear Fr Cajetan,

Mom's funeral Mass is on Tuesday at 10 am. I hope that you can be there to concelebrate. I have informed Wilma Brannan that you might be there. The Mass is at Blessed Sacrament.

Thank you Father. God bless!

MARY FADERAN

Mary

MOM'S LAST DAYS

March 25, 2011

Dear Ann,

My dearest Mom passed away this morning. God called her to His side and our Blessed Mother came to get her. My Dad and I stayed the night. Her heart stopped twice and after they resuscitated her the first time and vented her it stopped again and we told them to let her go. It is the Feast of the Annunciation, and I know that today God called her and she said her yes.

My Dad and I are in such sorrow but we know she is happy, free from the suffering she endured in her life. We take comfort knowing that God has rewarded her with a crown that each of us has waiting for us.

Thank you for your prayers for us.

Love,

Mary

MARY FADERAN

MOM'S LAST DAYS

March 25, 2011

Dear Fr Cajetan,

Mom's funeral Mass is on Tuesday at 10 am. I hope that you can be there to concelebrate. I have informed Wilma Brannan that you might be there. The Mass is at Blessed Sacrament.

Thank you Father. God bless!

Mary

March 25, 2011

Hello,

The visitation and rosary will be on Monday from 5 to 8 and Mass at 10:00 on Tuesday. Dad and I went to the funeral home today and the notice will be in tomorrow's paper. I wish we wrote of

MARY FADERAN

Mom's love for Jesus and Mother Mary in the obit but Dad and I were just not in our right thoughts. We are just feeling rudderless right now. Mom was our organizer, leader and focus and now that she's not with us it seems very surreal. Our trip to Walmart today seemed weird, and Dad commented that we won't be getting Mom's meds or Boost anymore. It was sad.

Well, I know many of you won't be able to come and we understand. We know that you would come if possible. Dad and I are just glad to know your thoughts and prayers are for us. We have been carried by them throughout Mom's struggles in the last few months. Thank you once again for your love and prayers and your words of comfort.

It's been a long day. I hope everyone has a restful weekend.

Love,

Mary

MOM'S LAST DAYS

March 25, 2011

Dear Janine,
Dad and I are ok right now. We are facing a very different night and days now without Mom. I know she is with us in spirit but I am craving the physical presence too. I know she wants us to join her when our time comes, and so I am now making sure that we follow her example because we know how she made it to heaven.

This weekend we will just do what's necessary. I'm not sure how the next week will go. As I said to Dad, we will take things a day at a time.

Love,
Mary

March 26, 2011

MARY FADERAN

Hi Jesty,
Thank you. We are grieving Mom but we also are glad that she is now in heaven and all her suffering has ended. Her death on the Feast of the Annunciation told us that God had willed this and the Blessed Mother herself came to take her home to heaven. So this fills my heart with joy and hope that everyone whose life she touched will be and is guarded by heaven and she is now more than ever praying for us to join her one day.
I heard that Sadira and Suzanne will fly out. Mom would be happy they are joining us.

March 26, 2011

Mary

Dear Letty and Cary,

Thank you so much. Mom is happy now, and we are comforted knowing this and so

MOM'S LAST DAYS

we feel better. We have been blessed with Mom's presence in our lives and thank God always for her as our beloved Mom and spouse. God has blessed us so much. Love is with us always now more than ever because her spirit lives on.

Blessings,

Mary and Don

MARY FADERAN

March 26, 2011

Dear Sr Ann,

It is what lifts me up - Mom's special departure on such a Holy Feast Day. I truly am so happy for her. We will have to be content in our diminished number.

Let us know when you will have time to meet us next week. We want to share our experience of Mom's passing with you.

Thank you once again, for your love and prayers.

Mary

MOM'S LAST DAYS

MARY FADERAN

March 26, 2011

Dear Bassy,

I am grateful to you for your prayers. Don't worry if you aren't able to come for the funeral. We are united in spirit and prayer wherever we are. Mom knows how you would have wanted to be here, and it is ok.

Our days have been a little better than expected since friends have come by and given us the warmth of food and friendship. It is good for us and Daddy especially to have good visits. I am hoping he will be able to cope with the absence of Mom in the time when I will be going back to work. The good thing is that at least I can come home for lunch and be with him.

Anyway, if you get a chance to call him once in a while, please do. His cell is -----.

MOM'S LAST DAYS

Love always,
Agnes

March 27, 2011

Marivic,'

Thanks so much. We are comforted by your prayers and know that she is watching over us, and being more effective in her prayers for us now that she is with God.

Mary

March 27, 2011

Dear Marilu,

MARY FADERAN

I can't believe that it is only 2 days since she passed away. Today we usually have our preparation to go to Mass. We went last night. I just don't think we could face our friends at Mass today and to be there without Mom for the first time. Yesterday wasn't too bad, some of our friends were there, and some of the Schoenstatt as well as Dad's friend from his work days. I look around at those who are my Mom's age and pray for them because they are so fragile and helpless and are just drawing near to their respective ends. I think that is a morbid thought but having come from the long days of the hospital with Mom, I just feel for them and their families. Even at the restaurant last night with a friend and Dad, there was a customer on her cell talking about her loved one going through a cat scan and I just prayed for them too. It still too fresh in my mind, and also in Dad's. I don't know how I can want to go to the hospital as a volunteer even now (I go volunteer at the Gift Shop once a month), knowing the place so well and each corner is like reminding me.

MOM'S LAST DAYS

Anyway, I hope to be busy today and not think so much about anything. I will be cleaning the house, some family is coming, although only one will be staying at home with us. The others are going to be at hotels, thank God. I am glad for the work to be done. Cannot sit and mope. Mom would not like that. I worry for Dad and how he is taking it. Please pray for him and his state of mind. I don't know how he will be when I have to go to work.

Thank you once again for your love and support and thoughts,

Mary

March 27, 2011

Hello Ro,

It was so good to see last night at Mass.

MARY FADERAN

Please know that I told Mom you were going to visit her and she seemed to understand and smile. She was still comprehending us even when she could not herself speak. I could tell she wanted us to stay that night before she died. I just wished that I had known for sure she would go and I would have stayed by her side all night long, instead of sleeping in the lounge down the hall. But Dad was with her in her room. They had her on a heart monitor and Dad had not realized her heart had stopped except when all the nurses ran into her room and told him and that was the start of her goodbye. I am really glad that I listened to Dr May who said that we will see how she goes through the night, and also how I felt that Mom wanted us to stay. She knew she was going to leave, and she was so loving in her gaze to us.

We will see you Monday and Tuesday then. God bless!

Mary

MOM'S LAST DAYS

March 27, 2011

Hello,

Just to let you know that I've attached a pdf of Mom's obit in yesterday's paper. I've already sent it to her brother, my Tito Nanding. Anyway, I hope that you can pray with us tomorrow at 5 pm EST and also on Tuesday morning at 10 a.m. for the Mass.

Love to you all, and thank you for your prayers and kind thoughts,

Mary

March 27, 2011

MARY FADERAN

Dear Tito Ding,

Thank you so much. Daddy and I are coping as well as we can with Mom's leaving. We are glad she no longer suffering and that now she has her heavenly body that keeps her closest to God. She died knowing we were there with her, hearing us tell her we love her. Now we just have to be strong and pray for the grace to carry on.

Love,

Agnes and Daddy

March 27, 2011

Hi Tito Nanding,

Please see the attached pdf file of Mom's obituary in yesterday's paper. I am having

MOM'S LAST DAYS

the funeral home assemble a DVD that has Mom's pictures. I will see if I can copy the DVD and send you the copy. Please feel free to send the attachment to our other relatives.

Thanks,

Agnes

March 27, 2011

Yes, that was her coding. She coded twice. The second time we asked them to let her go. We were with her at the end, and I think she knew we were with her, and that she heard us tell her how much we love her. I told her that we will see her again in heaven.

It has been such a long experience that I won't forget. I am glad that you were with us through it all, and that you were able to see her before she went. Thank you so much, Carole. I hope that you have a safe and happy trip.

See you when you come back.

Mary

March 28, 2011

Hi Valeria,

I want to let you know my Mom passed away last Friday. She had been ill for a few months and she was too

weakened to receive surgery. I and my Dad very sad but we know that the Blessed Mother came to take her to

Heaven on her feast day.

I hope that you and Rodolfo could say a prayer for her eternal rest.

MOM'S LAST DAYS

Yours in Jesus and Mary,

Mary

March 28, 2011

Janine,
If you think you want to bring something go ahead please. Mom touched the lives of many and I think more food is better than not enough. Besides Marichu and her team may be bringing Filipino dishes and American type food would be most welcome too.

Mary:)

March 28, 2011

Dear Drina,

MARY FADERAN

Thank you so much! We had the wake today and tons of people came, even the President of my company and my boss. It was just so good to see everyone. I am so tired now but tomorrow there's the Mass. My cousins from S Bend, Chicago and NY and the Salvo Girls-Suzanne, Sadira and Sandra- also came. Dad is feeling better but he is sad to lose Mom. I pray he will be able to look forward instead of backwards. Dear Drina I do miss you. Glenda came and Betina called.

I had better go. I will email a longer letter when things settle.

Love,
Mary

March 29, 2011

Hi Valeria,

MOM'S LAST DAYS

We are at home now. The Mass was so beautiful. She was laid to rest in a peaceful place.

We are consoled by the knowledge that she was received into heaven with the company of Our Lady on her special Feast Day.

Whenever Rodolfo would send Mom some of your family pictures, she beamed with joy.

Please call me --- anytime.

Mary

MARY FADERAN

April 3, 2011

Dear Ones,

Just wanted to thank you again for your generosity of time and financial help during our time of bereavement.

Erwin it was good to see you, and Dad has been lifted out of his grief when you were here.

Erv, thank you for the words of comfort and wisdom.

Eileen, thank you for being with me on the phone when we cried together.

Winnie, thank you for letting Erwin come out to be with us.

We are trying to live without Mom's presence now and it is a little strange. I am waking a little earlier now, and the first thought is Mom. I had a dream this

MOM'S LAST DAYS

morning of reading a letter from Mom but I couldn't figure out the words.

Anyway, I think she was close by. Eileen, maybe that was her telling me she was around, right?

I will let you guys know how we are from time to time. Tomorrow is back to work. Today we had brunch at friends' house. A good time. People there were from our Schoenstatt group and they said Mom is a saint. Now we are at

home, Dad is at the computer and I am curled up on the couch. We will go out again to get ink for the printer. Maybe hang at the BN cafe where I want to check out Gwyneth Paltrow's cookbook.

Love,

Ag

www.ingramcontent.com/pod-product-compliance
Lightning Source LLC
Chambersburg PA
CBHW051936290426
44110CB00015B/1999